Dynamic Antisymmetry

Adriana Picoral Scheidegger

adriana.picoral@gmail.com

Linguistic Inquiry Monographs
Samuel Jay Keyser, general editor

Dynamic Antisymmetry

Andrea Moro

The MIT Press
Cambridge, Massachusetts
London, England

This book was set in Times New Roman on '3B2' by Asco Typesetters, Hong Kong and was printed and bound in the United States of America.

Library of Congress Cataloging-in-Publication Data

Moro, Andrea.
  Dynamic antisymmetry / Andrea Moro.
    p.   cm. — (Linguistic inquiry monographs ; 38)
  Includes bibliographical references and index.
    ISBN 0-262-13375-X (alk. paper) — ISBN 0-262-63201-2 (pbk. : alk. paper)
    1. Generative grammar. I. Title. II. Series.
  P158.M65   2000
  415—dc21   00-040220

Adriana Picoral Scheidegger

adriana.picoral@gmail.com

Le signifiant, étant de nature auditive, se déroule dans le temps seul et a les caractères qu'il emprunte au temps: a) il représente une étendue, et b) cette étendue est mesurable dans une seule dimension: c'est une ligne. Ce principe est évident, mais il semble qu'on ait toujours négligé de l'énoncer, sans doute parce qu'on l'a trouvé trop simple; cependant il est fondamental et les conséquences en sont incalculables; ... Tout le mécanisme de la langue en dépend.

Ferdinand de Saussure

Contents

Chapter 4

Appendix

Series Foreword

We are pleased to present the thirty-eighth in the series *Linguistic Inquiry Monographs*. These monographs present new and original research beyond the scope of the article. We hope they will benefit our field by bringing to it perspectives that will stimulate further research and insight.

Originally published in a limited edition, the *Linguistic Inquiry Monographs* are now more widely available. This change is due to the great interest engendered by the series and by the needs of a growing readership. The editors thank the readers for their support and welcome suggestions about future directions for the series.

Samuel Jay Keyser
for the Editorial Board

Acknowledgments

The theory of Dynamic Antisymmetry results from the impact that Richard Kayne's and Noam Chomsky's reflections on language have had on me. I cannot imagine this work but as a comment on their seminal proposals.

I have presented Dynamic Antisymmetry during 1996 at the XXI Incontro di Grammatica Generativa (University of Bergamo), at the XIX GLOW Colloquium (University of Athens), at a seminar at the Istituto Scientifico H San Raffaele, and in talks at the City University of New York and MIT; during 1997 at the XXIII Incontro di Grammatica Generativa (Scuola Normale Superiore, Pisa), in a course I taught at the Landelijke Onderzoekschool Taalwetenschap (LOT) Winter School in Nijmegen, and at "Going Romance," the XI Symposium on Romance Linguistics (University of Groningen); during 1998 at a workshop at the University of Padua and at the conference "Inversion in Romance Languages" at the University of Amsterdam; and during 1999 in courses I taught at the Faculty of Psychology at the Università H San Raffaele and the GLOW International Summer School in Thermi, at a GLOW workshop, "Technical Aspects of Movement," at the University of Potsdam, and in talks at New York University, the Université du Québec à Montréal, McGill University, and the Lyon Institute of Cognitive Sciences. A first version of this theory circulated as an article in *Studia Linguistica* (Moro 1997a).

I am indebted to the audiences at the conferences and to the students in the courses I taught for many helpful comments. Special thanks to Carlo Cecchetto, Gennaro Chierchia, Noam Chomsky, Caterina Donati, Bob Frank, Giorgio Graffi, Richard Kayne, Giuseppe Longobardi, Massimo Piattelli-Palmarini, Luigi Rizzi, and two anonymous reviewers for their generous attention to this working hypothesis.

Introduction

Movement and the Linearization of Phrases

Displacement is a specific property of natural languages: certain constituents are interpreted in a position other than the one where they occur in the sequence of words. Considering the matter informally, let us look at a simple case.

(1) a. John believes that Mary knows [this story].
    b. [Which story] does John believe that Mary knows?

Even though the constituent *which story* does not follow *knows* in the sequence of words in (1b), it is interpreted as the object of *knows*, paralleling the case in (1a).

In transformational grammar, this core phenomenon is captured by assuming that constituents move from one position to another, within the limits imposed by a universal set of principles. This is represented by signaling the position from which the element moves with a symbol indicating an empty category, here the trace *t*.

(2) [Which story] does John believe that Mary knows t?

Another specific property of natural languages is phrase structure. Below the clause level, words are combined into recursive subunits, whose architecture is invariant across lexical and functional categories. Consider for example noun phrases in English.

(3)

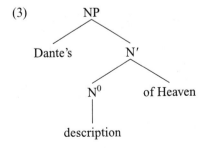

The head of the phrase, *description*, takes the phrase *of Heaven* as a complement, and the subphrase *description of Heaven* takes *Dante's* as a specifier, yielding the full noun phrase. Complements and specifiers can be construed according to the same architecture, yielding a uniform geometry.

In current theoretical frameworks it is generally assumed that these two properties are independent. On the one hand, movement has been related to morphology: phrases move to "check" their features in the proper morphological environment (see Chomsky 1993). On the other, phrase structure is derived by independent general principles governing either merging of lexical items (Chomsky 1995) or the mapping between hierarchy and linear order (Kayne 1994).

In this book I would like to suggest that movement and phrase structure are not independent. More specifically, I would like to suggest that movement is triggered by the geometry of phrase structure. To do so, I will adopt a weak version of Kayne's (1994) general theory of constituent structure, the *antisymmetry of syntax*. In this theory the complex architecture of phrases is traced back to a single principle, the Linear Correspondence Axiom (LCA), which maps hierarchy into linear precedence. Simplifying somewhat, Kayne proposes the following empirical hypothesis: "a word x precedes a word y if and only if a node X dominating x asymmetrically c-commands a node Y dominating y." The LCA derives all major properties of phrase structure: that each phrase must have a head, that each phrase can have only one head, that each head can have no more than one complement, and so on. Suppose for example that a phrase immediately contained two heads: there would be no way to organize the words dominated by the two heads in a sequence. In fact, the two heads would be at the same hierarchical level (call it a *point of symmetry*) and hence no precedence could be construed. Another assumption plays a fundamental role in Kayne's system: namely, that the LCA holds at all levels of representation. No point of symmetry can ever be generated.

My proposal is that the LCA is active only when needed—namely, at the interface with the articulatory-perceptual component (PF), where linearization of words into a sequence is required by definition. Prior to that point, syntactic trees are free to contain points of symmetry. Why should this weak version of the theory of antisymmetry bear on movement? The crucial observation is that traces are not visible to the PF component, independently of whether or not they are considered as copies; hence, they do not need to be linearized (see Kayne 1994, 133, n.3, Chomsky 1995, 337). Thus, movement can be thought of as a way to rescue the structure at PF in case a point of symmetry has been generated: since one of the elements constituting the point of symmetry is turned into an empty category (a trace), no problem arises for linearization. To put it more generally, movement turns out to be a consequence of the necessity of organizing words into a linear order. Let us call this theory *Dynamic Antisymmetry*. I will pursue the idea that all instances of movement in natural language are triggered by the geometry of phrase structure.

This book is organized as follows. Chapter 1 briefly outlines the current theory of movement. Chapter 2 illustrates aspects of the theory of anti-symmetry that are crucial to the Dynamic Antisymmetry proposal. Chapter 3 presents the empirical content of Dynamic Antisymmetry. Chapter 4 is very speculative and synthetic, addressing general questions about the overall design of grammar.

Chapter 3 deserves a preliminary, general observation. The hypothesis presented here potentially affects several heterogeneous domains of grammar—indeed, too many to be explored in a single work. My limited goal here is to suggest that the hypothesis offers a new perspective on two central aspects of the syntax of natural languages, movement and phrase structure—namely, that the former can be regarded as a function of the latter—and to illustrate some empirical and theoretical consequences of this point of view. To do so, I will concentrate on the syntax of raising in small clause constructions and on *wh*-movement in interrogatives (although I will also analyze other constructions such as clitic construc-tions in Italian). Indeed, we will see that Dynamic Antisymmetry allows the very notion of small clause to be refined, and that small clauses play a central role in more constructions than has generally been thought.

The data are taken mainly from English and Italian. To illustrate the core phenomena to which Dynamic Antisymmetry applies, an appendix presents the essentials of a unified theory of copular constructions stem-ming from my previous work in the field (Moro 1988, 1997b).

Chapter 1

Theories of Movement

All grammars must include some notion of displacement. To put it in Chomsky's words, the fact that some lexical items appear displaced from the position where they are interpreted is "an irreducible fact ... expressed somehow in every contemporary theory of language" (Chomsky 1995, 222).[1] In a multilevel grammar, for instance, displacement can be captured by assuming that a phrase moves from a given position at one level to a different position at another level.

Although the empirical issue is widely recognized, however, there is no general agreement on the nature of movement. As a matter of fact, the general issue is split into two distinct questions:[2] What are the formal mechanisms that underlie movement (i.e., how is movement actually triggered)? and Why do all and only human languages have this property?[3]

The first question has received several different answers that will be briefly reviewed here, ranging from Case-theoretical reasons to quantification (just to focus on movement of maximal projections). In general, researchers have concentrated on two conceptually distinct aspects of movement: establishing a typology of movement (distinguishing, e.g., between A- and Ā-movement or between X^0-movement and XP-movement), and developing a restrictive theory to reduce the power of movement transformations (i.e., locality theory; for a critical synopsis of different proposals ranging from Richard Kayne's Connectedness theory to Luigi Rizzi's Relativized Minimality, see Manzini 1992 and references cited there).

As for the second question, let us again consider Chomsky's words:

Why languages should have this property is an interesting question, which has been discussed for almost 40 years without resolution. My suspicion is that part of the reason has to do with phenomena that have been described in terms of surface structure interpretation, many of them familiar from traditional grammar: topic-comment, specificity, new and old information, the agentive force that we find even in displaced position and so on ... : it is motivated by interpretive requirements that are externally imposed by our systems of thought, which have these special properties, so the study of language use indicates. (Chomsky 1998; see also Chomsky 1995, 317; 1999, 3; 2000, 120–121)

Crucially, then, answering the second question would require exploring the conditions "externally imposed" by the interaction with performance systems in the sense specified within the Minimalist Program.

Before we look at the current theory of movement, a preliminary observation deserves highlighting. Although the questions of how and why movement is realized are conceptually distinct, it is clear that in the Minimalist Program a link is in fact established between the actual mechanisms of movement and the "extraneous conditions at the interface." The key notion is "interpretability." In the Minimalist Program this is captured by assuming a fundamental distinction within the morphological component: features are assumed to be either interpretable or uninterpretable at the relevant interface. A given feature's status might depend on the lexical item with which it is associated: for example, whereas Case is always uninterpretable, number is uninterpretable on a verb but interpretable on a noun. Movement is claimed to be driven by the necessity of deleting a given item's uninterpretable features.

Since the very first proposal, different ways of accomplishing deletion of uninterpretable features have been suggested (for a brief sketch, see section 1.3.1). In general, however, all approaches assume that deletion of features requires "pairing" of identical (types of) features. At an informal level the mechanism of movement can be synthetically described as follows. Whenever a lexical item containing an uninterpretable feature is introduced into the derivation, for the sentence to converge the system requires an item containing the same (type of) feature to enter into a local relation with it. One possible way to construe such a relation is to move one item containing a feature φ, typically a phrase, from a local domain to enter into a spec(ifier)-head relation with a head containing the same feature φ; this causes the feature to delete by definition.

From this perspective movement is nothing but a device to wipe out uninterpretable entities at the relevant interface (see Chomsky 1995, 278). As the discussion proceeds, it will be important to recall that the notion of interpretability inherently relies on conditions that are extraneous to syntax in the broad sense.

1.1 Empirical Evidence for Movement

To begin, let us address a very basic question: how do we know that a certain constituent has been moved? Here we face a paradox typical of many issues in linguistics. On the one hand, we have a strong intuition of what movement is. On the other, once we attempt to characterize movement from a theoretical point of view, many problems arise requiring commitment on fundamental issues.

The basic intuition by which we judge that an item has moved is essentially distributional. Consider again a typical example.

(1) a. John believes that Mary knows [this story].

b. [Which story] does John believe that Mary knows?

We assume that *which story* has been moved from the object position of *knows* in (1b) for two reasons: a phrase belonging to the same category as *which story*—namely, *this story*—can occur as the object of *knows* in (1a), and *which story* is in fact interpreted as the object of *knows*. But why can we not assume that the reverse movement took place—namely, that *this story* in (1a) has been moved from the position where *which story* occurs in (1b)? Clearly, we have no immediate or mechanical answer to this question, although from an intuitive point of view we feel that the second alternative is not plausible. In fact, since the very first attempts to define movement transformations (Chomsky 1957) it has been clear that the reasons for assuming when and what movement has taken place cannot be merely distributional; rather, they must crucially rely on psychological considerations, simplicity, naturalness, plausibility on acquisitional grounds, and so on. More generally, it is clear that there can be no automatic procedure for discovering movement; the typical method of scientific inquiry is required, making crucial use of hypotheses and experiments for each case and evaluating the results on global grounds.

Given these premises, one can at least descriptively distinguish different types of evidence in favor of movement by relying on standard grammatical apparatus and terminology. Thus, one type of evidence is based on θ-relations (long-distance predicate-argument relations such as those in *wh*-constructions, raising, passive, clitic constructions, etc.). A second type is based on binding theory (crossover effects, reconstruction phenomena, etc.). A third type is related to LF properties (scopal readings, quantification, saturation, etc.). A fourth type is found in the distribution of functional elements and expletives in both clauses and noun phrases (verb-second phenomena, expletive replacement, N^0-to-D^0 raising, etc.). Finally, movement can be assumed for purely theory-internal reasons, as in the case of the "vacuous movement hypothesis" discussed in Chomsky 1986a, 48ff. There Chomsky considers whether the subject *who* moves from preverbal position to the specifier of CP or stays in situ in the specifier of IP in root sentences like (2).

(2) Who fixed the car in this way?

Clearly, (2) provides no compelling argument based on θ-relations, binding theory, or LF properties; it is compatible with the hypothesis that *who* has never moved from the subject position. An argument for assuming that *who* moves comes from comparing (2) with a different structure.

(3) *How do you wonder [who fixed the car t]?

If *who* in (2) were not raised to the specifier of CP of the inner clause, occupying the only possible escape hatch from which to exit the embedded clause, there would be no reason why *how* should yield such Empty Category Principle–like violations as (3).[4]

Indeed, the discovery over the years that all the heterogeneous classes of phenomena mentioned here are governed by the same theory of locality has provided strong, although indirect, support for the very existence of movement.

In sum, a major point concerning theories of movement is that the identification of movement, the typology of movement, and the mechanisms that underlie movement can be determined only by choosing a specific theory. Thus, although certain phenomena (e.g., in interrogatives) are recognized generally as instances of movement, a given theory might not include other phenomena (e.g., stylistic movement, prosody-related phenomena, and "scrambling") in the domain of movement proper. This has indeed characterized research in transformational grammar from the earliest moments to the present:

In early transformational grammar, a distinction was sometimes made between "stylistic" rules and others. Increasingly, the distinction seems to be quite real: the core computational properties we have been considering differ markedly in character from many other operations of the language faculty, and it may be a mistake to try to integrate them within the same framework of principles. The problems related to XP-adjunction are perhaps a case in point ... (Chomsky 1995, 324–325)

Whether or not restricting attention to "narrow syntax" is a correct move can only be decided on empirical grounds, by considering grammar as a whole. Bearing these general issues in mind, we will concentrate on two core syntactic phenomena that nowadays are undisputedly considered as involving movement: Case assignment and *wh*-constructions.[5]

1.2 Toward a Morphological Account: Case Assignment and *Wh*-Movement

Case assignment and *wh*-movement were originally studied separately and captured by two conceptually distinct devices: the Case Filter and the *Wh*-Criterion, respectively. From a theoretical point of view, the essential difference between a filter and a criterion is that a criterion is a filter including a one-to-one mapping between a (feature contained in a) head and a (feature contained in a) phrase. More specifically, in the most advanced formulations a criterion requires a spec-head relation between two elements containing the same type of feature. For example, criteria have been proposed for θ-relations (see Chomsky 1981, 36), *wh*-movement (see Rizzi 1996 and references cited there), and negation (see Haegeman and Zanuttini 1991).

The reduction of Case assignment to spec-head agreement between a phrase and (a head containing) an Agr^0 has led to a unified analysis of these phenomena, for it has become possible to consider Case assignment as a particular instance of a more general class of phenomena that includes *wh*-movement. Prior to the so-called split-Infl hypothesis (see Pollock 1989 and independently Moro 1988), it was not conceptually possible to reduce Case assignment to a criterion, since, for example, accusative Case was not assigned in a spec-head relation; rather, it was assigned under government by the lexical verb. After the split-Infl hypothesis stemming from Pollock's work was extended to include an independent head for object agreement (i.e., $Agr^0{}_O$; see Kayne 1989, Belletti 1990, Chomsky 1993 (the last two crucially relying on Baker's (1988) Mirror Principle), and many related works), it became possible to reduce the Case Filter to a criterion. Nominative and accusative Case turned out to be (associated to) the same type of structure: a spec-head relation with an abstract Agr^0.

(4)   AgrP

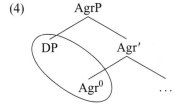

The difference between nominative and accusative then reflected the different components of the head resulting from incorporation of Agr^0: accusative when V^0 is incorporated into Agr^0_O, yielding $[V^0\text{-}Agr^0_O]$, and nominative when $[[V^0\text{-}Agr^0_O]\ T^0]$ is incorporated into Agr^0_S. Although the most recent versions of the Minimalist Program (since Chomsky 1995) no longer make use of Agr^0 heads, the same type of structure essentially persists. Even if Agr^0 does not mediate the relation and Case is checked rather than assigned, a spec-head relation must occur between a DP and a head containing the relevant feature (either T^0 or v; see Chomsky 1995, 2000), possibly including multiple adjunction to the same phrase (multiple-spec constructions) and expletive insertion.[6]

The unification of *wh*-movement and Case assignment had an important theoretical consequence for the overall design of the grammar. Since all criteria depend on morphological properties, it was hypothesized that all movements are driven by morphological requirements only. Within the Minimalist Program this hypothesis has become the central assumption about movement, one that plays a crucial role in understanding the nature of human language. In this book an alternative approach will be proposed that does not directly link movement to morphology.

1.3   (Im)perfections of Language

Admittedly, minimalism is so far a way to look at the structure of human language, rather than a specific formal system. Indeed, there are different ways of positing minimality in grammar: it can bear on the amount of structure that can be involved in computation (economy of derivation);[7] on the effort to minimize the number of abstract entities used in the explanation, such as functional heads (Ockham's razor); or on the number of levels of representation, which are reduced to the interfaces with performance systems of the mind/brain ("biologically oriented" minimalism). It is the third way of interpreting minimalism that is relevant here.

More precisely, within the Minimalist Program only two levels of representation are assumed: Phonetic Form (PF) and Logical Form (LF). These are the interface levels with the two necessary components of the human mind: the articulatory-perceptual component and the conceptual-intentional component, respectively. According to this view, all principles are established as "legibility conditions" at either level (LF or PF), in the sense that principles must ensure that linguistic expressions can be properly read as "instructions" by the performance systems.[8] These legibility conditions have been called *bare output conditions*. Within this framework, since the appearance of Chomsky 1993, it has been possible to approach the question "Why is there movement?" in an unprecedented way. In the next section I will briefly illustrate some core aspects of a minimalist theory of movement, concentrating on their general consequences.

1.3.1 Two Apparent Imperfections

Sound and meaning features are assembled and then paired to form lexical items. In a perfect design for language all features would be interpretable (at the proper interface). Within the Minimalist Program human languages are considered imperfect in that not all features are interpretable; specifically, certain inflectional features such as (structural) Case features are assumed not to be interpretable at LF. Displacement also seems unnecessary: why should certain constituents move from the position where they are inserted in the course of derivation? Apparently, then, movement is to be regarded as a second basic imperfection of human language. Must we conclude that human language indeed contains two such imperfections? According to Chomsky, if we look at these two facts in isolation, the answer is affirmative, but if we examine the interaction between uninterpretable features and movement, we will reach the non-obvious conclusion that language contains no imperfections at all (see, e.g., Chomsky 1995, 317; 1999, 3; 2000, sec. 3.5). To understand this conclusion, we must preliminarily understand the interaction between features and movement from a technical point of view.

The central thesis of the minimalist theory of movement is that movement is a way grammar avoids presenting the interfaces with uninterpretable features contained in the lexicon. In other words, within the Minimalist Program the two imperfections appear to be intimately, although not necessarily, related: if there were no uninterpretable features, there would be no movement. This hypothesis is crucially based on two assumptions: first, obviously, there are uninterpretable features; second, a feature can be deleted only in a proper local configuration with another feature of the same type. I will not discuss here whether these two assumptions are empirically and theoretically justified. My limited aim is to consider how the system works. The mechanism is essentially this: any (item containing an) uninterpretable formal feature that is introduced into the derivation must be "paired" before reaching LF with (another item containing) the same type of feature in a local relation; this is what deletes the uninterpretable feature.[9] The question now is how "pairing" is implemented in syntax.

As noted in section 1.2, within the minimalist framework there have been three versions (corresponding to Chomsky 1993, 1995, 2000) of what the proper local relation is that can perform deletion, and the technical proposals are developing rapidly. In all versions, however, the crucial assumption that the system deletes uninterpretable features by pairing them in the proper local configuration has remained constant. Let us briefly review them. There is a sharp technical difference between the first and second versions. In the first version Agr^0 played a central role in the "pairing-deletion" process: "The function of Agr is to provide a structural configuration in which features can be checked ..." (Chomsky 1995, 351). Leaving aside questions related to the strength of features,[10] at LF the subject and the object DP in all transitive sentences were said to move to a distinct specifier of AgrP position to ensure deletion of the uninterpretable feature. In the second version Agr^0 heads were no longer available, having been eliminated from Universal Grammar. In this version the process of deletion involved raising to the extant clausal functional categories, namely, T^0 and the light verb v (see Chomsky 1995, sec. 4.10.2). At this stage movement could be overt (involving the whole phrase) or covert (involving the relevant features only). Since then the system has been further simplified: feature movement has been abandoned, by decomposing movement into two more primitive operations, Merge and Agree. Merge is the usual operation of composition of phrases (I will come back to it in chapter 3); Agree establishes a relation between two items (a probe and a goal) in some restricted search space (Chomsky 2000, 119ff.). Thus, the operation Move establishes agreement via merging a copy of the relevant item in the proper local specifier position, performing deletion of uninterpretable features. Alternatively, deletion can be accomplished via merging of an expletive or without merging simply by application of Agree alone. The choice among alternatives, of course, is not casual.

Plainly Move is more complex than its subcomponents Merge and Agree, or even the combination of the two, since it involves the extra step of determining P(F) [a phrase determined by a feature F] (generalized "pied-piping"). Good design conditions would lead us to expect that simpler operations are preferred to more complex ones, so that Merge or Agree (or their combination) preempts Move, which is a "last resort," chosen when nothing else is possible. (Chomsky 2000, 101–102; see also Chomsky 1999, 4)

Notably, in this version, although the process still affects features, the mechanism of movement operates on full constituents (heads and their projections) rather than features themselves, thus excluding covert movement of features.[11]

Synthesizing, although the different versions of the mechanism yielding feature pairing in the minimalist framework may yield substantial differences, both empirical and theoretical, there is at least one constant assumption that holds throughout the whole development of the theory and is surely worth emphasizing here: movement is driven by the necessity of deleting uninterpretable features, in that it provides a proper local relation (when other options are excluded).

Let us now return to the main issue of this section: the consequences of the interaction between uninterpretable features and movement for the overall design of grammar. Chomsky (2000, 120) introduces this issue best.

[W]e have two "imperfections" to consider: uninterpretable features and the dislocation property. These properties (in fact, morphology altogether) are never built into special-purpose symbolic systems. We might suspect, then, that they have to do with externally imposed legibility conditions. With regard to dislocation, that has been suggested from the earliest days of modern generative grammar, with speculations about facilitation of processing (on the sound side) and the dissociation of "deep" and "surface" interpretive principles (on the meaning side).

The answer then is clear: natural language is not imperfect at all, at least with respect to the two potential imperfections examined here. Imperfections appear only if we consider two properties in isolation; whenever we look at the system where they interact as whole, the imperfections appear to yield a welcome perfect solution to the necessity imposed by legibility conditions on the external systems.

1.3.2 The Other Side of Bare Output Conditions

The central claim I will address in this book is that we can dispense with the morphological explanation for movement described above, that is, with the assumption that movement is forced so that LF receives no structures containing uninterpretable features. As for the existence and the role of uninterpretable features in syntax, I leave this issue open as one that does not bear on movement.[12]

In the minimalist framework all conditions must be related to either LF or PF, the two biologically necessary interface levels. Movement has been related to LF, as a reflex of Full Interpretation, the principle requiring that no uninterpretable feature feed the conceptual-intentional component. In the alternative proposal that I will suggest here, the principles forcing movement are still related to only one of the two necessary levels, but it is the opposite one, namely, PF. In other words, movement is still regarded as a way to meet the bare output conditions of an interface level, as in the standard minimalist framework; the difference is that the relevant interface is the one facing the articulatory-perceptual performance system. These views become possible if we adopt a weak version of Kayne's (1994) theory of the antisymmetry of syntax.

Chapter 2

Movement as a Symmetry-Breaking Phenomenon

Dynamic Antisymmetry will be presented in two steps. Section 2.1 briefly illustrates the original version of the antisymmetry of syntax (Kayne 1994), concentrating on crucial aspects of the theory. Section 2.2 introduces the alternative theory of movement based on weak antisymmetry, preparing for the discussion of empirical data in chapter 3.

2.1 Hierarchy and Precedence: The Linear Correspondence Axiom

The antisymmetry of syntax is a theory of phrase structure based on the Linear Correspondence Axiom (LCA). Let us first consider this theory from a rather informal point of view. Linguistic expressions have, so to speak, two distinct "dimensions": the bare linear dimension where words are organized in sequences at PF, and the hierarchical dimension of phrase structure where grammatical relations (e.g., binding, agreement, θ-role assignment, government) are established. If it were not for the necessity of linearizing words at PF, grammatical relations could be expressed solely by means of hierarchical relations.[1] In general, linear order has always been thought of as independent from hierarchy. From a purely combinatorial point of view, for any given triple of words—say, w, w', and w''—the sequence $ww'w''$ can have the hierarchical structures shown in (1).

(1) a.   b.   c.

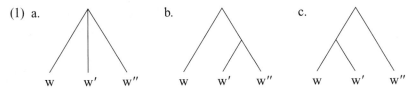

The possibility of a "flat" structure such as (1a) has been refuted by Kayne (1984, 133), who proposed that each node can have at most two branches (Binary Branching Principle). Nevertheless, it has always been assumed that (1b) and (1c) are both possible phrase structures for the same sequence.

The independence of linear order and hierarchy has led to the formulation of linearization parameters, including the so-called head-complement parameter according to which the linear order of the complement and the head of a phrase is parametrically fixed in a unique way for all types of phrases in a given language (see Van Riemsdijk 1978, Graffi 1980 for earlier proposals; see also Chomsky 1986a,b and references cited there for the standard view). Let us consider the situation from the most general point of view. A phrase projected from any head X^0 has the universal hierarchical structure shown in (2) (where "(a, b)" is the unordered pair of a and b and Z'' (ZP) and Y'' (YP) are construed recursively according to the same schema as X'' (XP)).

(2) a. $X'' = (X', Z'')$
    b. $X' = (X^0, Y'')$

This simple representation contains several pieces of information: it requires that a phrase contain a head, that there be only one head per phrase, that a head not have a head as a complement, and so on. The grammar of each language, then, must include a specific instruction that fixes the linear order of phrases in one of the four possible combinations (where "$\langle a, b \rangle$" is the ordered pair of a and b meaning "a precedes b").

(3) a. i. $X'' = \langle Z'', X' \rangle$
       ii. $X' = \langle X^0, Y'' \rangle$
    b. i. $X'' = \langle Z'', X' \rangle$
       ii. $X' = \langle Y'', X^0 \rangle$
    c. i. $X'' = \langle X', Z'' \rangle$
       ii. $X' = \langle X^0, Y'' \rangle$
    d. i. $X'' = \langle X', Z'' \rangle$
       ii. $X' = \langle Y'', X^0 \rangle$

Prototypical examples are considered to be English and Romance languages for (3a), Japanese and Turkish for (3b), Malagasy for (3c) (see Longobardi 1990). Immediately, an obvious question arises: why is type (3d) not realized? In fact, other problems show up as well. If we look inside the structure of noun phrases, Italian appears to be a class (3c) language as well (see Giorgi and Longobardi 1991); researchers are currently debating whether Dutch verb phrases are head initial or head final (see Zwart 1997 and references cited there); and many other cases could also be cited. All in all, one important observation emerges: as soon as the analysis is refined, the generalizations synthesized in the standard X-bar theory, including many of Greenberg's (1963) original generalizations, are too rigid as stated.[2]

Kayne's (1994) theory departs radically from this approach by proposing that the two dimensions, linear and hierarchical, are interlocked in a nontrivial way. More specifically, the LCA is an empirical hypothesis regarding Universal Grammar to the effect that for any given hierarchy, precedence is fixed in a unique way for all languages; in other words, for (2a–b) there is only one choice among the options in (3). This theory has many deep and intricate consequences, both theoretical and empirical, which it is not possible to discuss here. Essentially, the consequences of the LCA fall into two groups: formal (i.e., the LCA derives all of the instructions characterizing phrase structure: one head per phrase, binary branching, etc.) and comparative (i.e., the LCA drastically reduces the available options across languages, solving many of the problems left unanswered by the standard model, including the ones noted above). The effects on the comparative issue are exemplified in the following quotation:

If languages were allowed the option of having complements precede heads and heads precede specifiers, then we would expect to find languages that were the mirror image of Germanic with respect to verb-second phenomena (i.e., the finite verb would move to second-from-last position in root sentences). I do not know of any such languages. If that gap is not accidental, it supports the idea that S-H-C [specifier-head-complement] is the only available order of constituents. (Kayne 1994, 50)

Indeed, if hierarchy were totally independent of linear order, such a gap, and many more, would be very hard to justify.

Clearly, a major cost of the LCA is that linearization parameters such as the head-complement parameter must be excluded from Universal Grammar. The observed variations must be discharged to some other component of grammar via transformations. At present this issue constitutes a major and surely challenging field of research (see, e.g., Kayne 1998 and references cited there).

We will approach the comparative issue (marginally) in chapter 4. For now, since the alternative theory of movement presented here crucially relies on the LCA, we must look at its technical and core aspects. Let us preliminarily approach the question from a rather abstract point of view, beginning with a few technical notions. The first is "relation."[3] What is a relation? Intuitively, it is something that may hold between concrete or abstract individuals in the world: the relation "being the spouse of" holds between men and women, the relation "being a multiple of" holds between integers, and so on. Technically, there are two fundamental ways to denote a relation: either by giving a list of ordered pairs of elements for which the relation holds or by stating a rule for finding whether for any two elements of a given domain, the relation holds. In set-theoretic terms, a relation can be represented as a subset of the set consisting of all ordered pairs (written as "$\langle a, b \rangle$") of elements belonging to two given sets (called the "Cartesian product" of the sets). A relation can hold between objects of two different sets A and B (a relation *from* A to B) or between objects of the same set A (a relation *in* A). Of course, a relation can be generalized as consisting of sets of ordered sets of triples, quadruples, and so on. In fact, binary relations can have special properties that are usually given special names. For example, a relation R is called "transitive" if and only if for all ordered pairs $\langle x, y \rangle$ and $\langle y, z \rangle$, $\langle x, z \rangle$ is also in R; a relation R is called "antisymmetric" if and only if it is never the case that for any $\langle x, y \rangle$ in R, $\langle y, x \rangle$ is also in R; a relation R in A is "total" if and only if for any distinct elements of A, x and y, either $\langle x, y \rangle$ or $\langle y, x \rangle$.[4] Of course, these properties can hold separately; however, since a relation where they occur together plays an important role in many fields, it is standardly given a special name. Thus, following Kayne's (1994) terminology, we can define a *linear ordering* as a special binary relation that has these three properties:

(4) a. It is transitive.
    b. It is total.
    c. It is antisymmetric.

Are there linear orderings in syntax? Assuming the familiar distinction between terminal nodes and nonterminal nodes in phrase markers, precedence is obviously a linear ordering defined on the set of terminals:[5] if a terminal node x precedes a terminal node y and the terminal node y precedes a terminal node z, then the terminal node x precedes the terminal node z (transitivity); and so on. The reverse of precedence (subsequence) is also a linear ordering on the set of terminals: if a terminal node x follows a terminal node y and the terminal node y follows a terminal node z, then the terminal node x follows the terminal node z (transitivity); and so on. Now, is linear ordering also defined on the set of nonterminals? Consider the hierarchical relation of c-command, adopting a simple definition close to Reinhart's (1976) original proposal.

(5) A c-commands B if and only if
   a. A does not dominate B;
   b. the first node dominating A also dominates B.

This is a relation on the set of nonterminals; it is transitive, but it is of course neither antisymmetric (in a tree, distinct nonterminal nodes can c-command each other) nor total (in a tree, there can be two nodes neither of which c-commands the other). Let us now restrict c-command to asymmetric c-command.

(6) A asymmetrically c-commands B if and only if
   A c-commands B and B does not c-command A.

Now the relation is transitive and antisymmetric by definition. However, it is still not total. It becomes total whenever it is restricted to the set of nodes c-commanding a given node: "in a binary branching tree, if Y asymmetrically c-commands X and Z (distinct from Y) also asymmetrically c-commands X, then it must be the case that either Y asymmetrically c-commands Z or Z asymmetrically c-commands Y" (Kayne 1994, 4–5). In such a case we call the asymmetric c-command a *locally linear ordering* on the set of nonterminals.

We now have all the tools to express the LCA. We will approach the definition of the LCA step by step, keeping in mind that this axiom interlocks nonterminal and terminal nodes. As a first step, let us consider the LCA from an informal point of view: "The intuition that I would like to pursue is that there should be a very close match between the linear ordering relation on the set of terminals and some comparable relation on nonterminals. By *comparable*, I now mean locally linear" (Kayne 1994, 5). We can now define *close match* formally. The familiar notion "dominance" will mediate the matching between the locally linear order of antisymmetric c-command defined on nonterminals and the linear order of precedence defined on terminals. Let us define the dominance relation g from the set of nonterminals to the set of terminals as follows:

(7) For a given nonterminal X, g(X) is the set of terminals that X dominates.

We can also define a dominance relation d from the set of ordered pairs of nonterminals (the Cartesian product of nonterminals) to the set of ordered pairs of terminals (the Cartesian product of terminals). One possibility is that d is simply based on g.

(8) For a given pair of nonterminals $\langle X, Y \rangle$, $d(\langle X, Y \rangle)$ is the set of ordered pairs $\langle x, y \rangle$ such that x is a member of $g(X)$ and y is a member of $g(Y)$.

We can now capture formally the intuition that asymmetric c-command is closely matched to the linear ordering of terminals. Let us restrict ourselves to the subset of the Cartesian product of nonterminals that is the relation of asymmetric c-command, calling it A. More specifically, for a given syntactic tree, let A be the biggest set of pairs of nonterminals $\langle X, Y \rangle$ such that X c-commands Y but Y does not c-command X. The LCA can be simply stated as a condition on d(A).

(9) *LCA*

d(A) is a linear ordering.

The LCA interlocks terminals and nonterminals in a straightforward way by associating one and only one linear ordering of terminals to any given hierarchy.[6] Another way to put it is to consider, so to speak, the "reversed" path that led to d(A): "the LCA, by virtue of requiring *d* (the dominance relation between nonterminals and terminals) to map *A* into a linear ordering, has forced the set of nonterminals to inherit the antisymmetry of the linear ordering of the terminals" (Kayne 1994, 9). A core assumption of the LCA to which I return in section 2.2 is that it cannot be violated at any syntactic level: in other words, the LCA is active before and after Spell-Out, regardless of whether one assumes a derivational or a representational point of view.

There is only one thing to be added here. As noted earlier, there are two linear orderings defined on terminal nodes: precedence and subsequence. In fact, d could map the antisymmetric relation on nonterminals (asymmetric c-command) into either precedence or subsequence. Kayne (1994, sec. 4.3) claims that there are empirical reasons that force antisymmetric c-command to map into precedence. I will depart here from Kayne's theory and simply assume that precedence is universally selected.

To summarize thus far: The LCA is an empirical hypothesis according to which the locally linear ordering of nonterminals is mapped onto the linear ordering of terminals in a unique way. If a node X asymmetrically c-commands a node Y, all terminals dominated by X precede all terminals dominated by Y. Conversely, if a terminal node x precedes a terminal node y, there must be a nonterminal node X dominating x that asymmetrically c-commands at least one nonterminal node Y dominating y. This is essentially the formal content of the LCA. I will now illustrate some consequences of adopting the LCA.

As noted earlier, the LCA is able to derive all major properties of the architecture of phrases. Following Kayne, let us preliminarily consider structures quite abstractly by representing nonterminal nodes and terminal nodes with capital and lowercase letters, respectively. (10) shows the representation of two terminals, x and y, and their relation to the nonterminals that dominate them, X and Y.

(10)

How many (minimal) combinations are possible under the LCA? First consider the easy case, where X c-commands Y but Y does not c-command X, as in (11).

(11)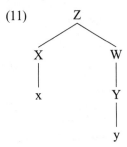

Clearly, this simple tree satisfies the LCA. Specifically, x precedes y because there is an ordered pair of nonterminals $\langle X, Y \rangle$ such that the first member c-commands the second but the second does not c-command the first. Thus, d maps $\langle X, Y \rangle$ into $\langle x, y \rangle$, which is interpreted as 'x precedes y'. (The fact that X and W do c-command each other is irrelevant here. Neither $\langle X, W \rangle$ nor $\langle W, X \rangle$ is in A, that is, the set of pairs of nonterminals such that the first element c-commands the second but not vice versa. With regard to (11), then, A consists only of the pair $\langle X, Y \rangle$.)

Now consider the representation in (12), graphically the mirror image of (11).

(12)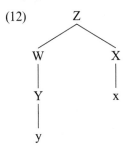

The hierarchical (i.e., c-command) relations between nonterminals are the
same as in (11). Thus, d maps $\langle X, Y \rangle$ into $\langle x, y \rangle$, which is interpreted
as 'x precedes y', exactly as before. The fact that (11) and (12) look dif-
ferent is related to the necessity of representing syntactic structures on
a plane: one direction of branching must be chosen for purely physical
reasons.

To complete this brief illustration of the LCA, let us look at the case
where X and Y do c-command each other. Consider the representation (13).

(13)

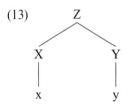

This tree is not compatible with the LCA. There is no way to put x and y
into a linear order because the tree contains no pair of nonterminals such
that the first c-commands the second but the second does not c-command
the first. In other words, A is empty; thus, d(A) is also empty. Let us call
the offending (unordered) pair (X, Y) a *point of symmetry*.

Let us now translate these abstract representations into the more usual
terminology of X-bar theory. Any nonterminal node immediately dominating a terminal node is a *head*. From this perspective, (13) is impossible
because the head of a phrase Z (which we can assume to be a projection
of either X or Y) cannot take another head as a sister. In fact, (13) would
become LCA compatible if more structure were added, yielding (11) or
equivalently (12). Notice, however, that simply adding "more structure"
to (13) does not necessarily make it LCA compatible. Consider structure (14).

(14)

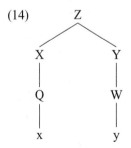

We must be careful here. As in (13), X and Y mutually c-command each other and thus cannot be invoked to linearize the set of terminals (in other words, neither the pair $\langle X, Y \rangle$ nor the pair $\langle Y, X \rangle$ is in A). However, A is not empty: there is a nonterminal node X containing x that asymmetrically c-commands a nonterminal node W containing y. Thus, the pair $\langle X, W \rangle$ appears to enable x and y to be linearly ordered. But the appearance is deceiving since there is also a pair of nonterminals $\langle Y, Q \rangle$ such that the first member c-commands the second but the second does not c-command the first; thus, $\langle Y, Q \rangle$ is also in A. In fact, if we map A under d onto the Cartesian product of terminal nodes, we have the following result. From the pairs of nonterminals $\langle X, W \rangle$ and $\langle Y, Q \rangle$, we obtain that the pairs of terminals $\langle x, y \rangle$ and $\langle y, x \rangle$ are both in d(A); thus, it is the case both that x precedes y and that y precedes x. This disqualifies d(A) as a linear ordering because antisymmetry is not respected. Again, the offending (unordered) pair (X, Y) is a point of symmetry. Translated into X-bar terminology, this conclusion about the abstract representation in (14) amounts to excluding that two projections can be merged unless a head intervenes. This immediately raises an obvious question concerning specifiers and adjuncts in general. Let us first approach the issue from an abstract point of view, as usual.

Let us modify one of our well-formed trees, (11), as in (15).

(15)

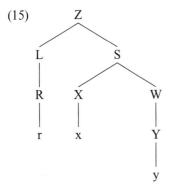

This tree is not LCA compatible. Under the definition of c-command adopted here, (L, S) is a point of symmetry: neither x nor y can be linearized with respect to r. The set A contains $\langle L, X \rangle$, $\langle L, W \rangle$, $\langle L, Y \rangle$, and $\langle S, R \rangle$. Under d, these pairs give $\langle r, x \rangle$, $\langle r, y \rangle$, $\langle r, y \rangle$, $\langle x, r \rangle$, and $\langle y, r \rangle$. Since d(A) contains both $\langle r, x \rangle$ and $\langle x, r \rangle$ (and both $\langle r, y \rangle$ and $\langle y, r \rangle$), the relation is not antisymmetric and d(A) does not qualify as a linear ordering. Is this a welcome result? There are reasons to conclude that it is not. In X-bar terms, excluding (15) amounts to excluding a simple tree where $X = X^0$, $S = X'$, and $Z = XP$. This is clearly an unwelcome result: specifiers would always constitute a point of symmetry with the phrase they are merged to. To solve this problem, Kayne suggests relying on the distinction between segments and categories and redefining c-command accordingly. This distinction, introduced by May (1985) and adopted by Chomsky (1986b), regards categories as being composed of segments. Thus, for example, when an element α is adjoined to category X, we say that category X is extended; that is, another segment of it is added, yielding [x α X]. Kayne proposes defining c-command in terms of the category/segment distinction (see Kayne 1994, 16).

(16) X c-commands Y if and only if
    a. X and Y are categories,
    b. no segments of X dominate Y,
    c. every category that dominates X dominates Y.

Now consider (17), differing minimally from (15) in that adjunction of L to category Z is manifested by the double occurrence of the label Z; that is, category Z has been enriched by one segment.

(17)

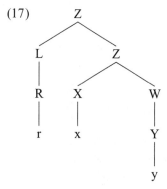

The structure is now fully compatible with the LCA. Category Z, consisting of the two distinct segments Z, does not c-command L, because one segment of Z dominates L (violating (16b)); the lower segment of Z cannot c-command any node because it is not a category (as required by (16a)). On the other hand, ⟨L, X⟩ is in A (and ⟨L, W⟩, ⟨L, Y⟩ are in A), with the result that r precedes x (and y). Again, notice that (18), where L is to the right of the lowest segment of Z, is entirely equivalent to (17), from the point of view of the linear order of the set of terminals, since the c-command relations are exactly the same as those in (17).

(18)

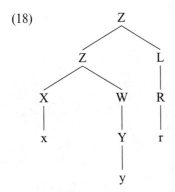

Thus, under the new definition of c-command, adjuncts are allowed. What can we say about specifiers? In fact, the new definition of c-command unifies specifiers and adjuncts as the same sort of entity.[7] "Unless there turns out to be another natural way to permit specifiers within the theory developed here, the conclusion must be that a specifier is necessarily to be taken as an adjoined phrase, involving crucial use of the segment/category distinction" (Kayne 1994, 17). The impossibility of merging a further maximal projection to (17), or equivalently (18), can be illustrated as follows.

Let us make (17) more complex, as in (19). Again, it does not matter whether the new segment is represented on the left or on the right; here it is represented on the right.

(19)

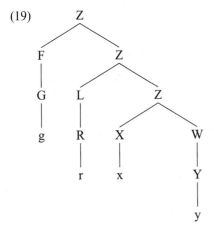

Is this tree compatible with the LCA? Given the definition of c-command adopted here, F and L c-command each other. The situation parallels the one in (14); that is, (F, L) is a point of symmetry. We conclude that the LCA implies that at most one specifier/adjunct is allowed per head.[8]

Limiting ourselves to looking at the LCA-compatible structures, we can see that most stipulated properties of X-bar theories—in particular, the ones listed in (20)—can be derived from the LCA. In what follows I will rely heavily on the schema given in Cinque 1996, 449ff. (from which (20) and (21) are quoted).

(20) a. There can be no phrase dominating two (or more) phrases (Kayne (199[4]): 11).
   b. There cannot be more than one head per phrase (Kayne (199[4]): 8).
   c. A head cannot take another head as a complement (Kayne (199[4]): 8).
   d. A head cannot have more than one complement (Kayne (199[4]): 136, fn. 28).

Along with these standard properties of X-bar theories, the following special properties can also be derived from the LCA (via the definition of c-command based on the segment/category distinction):

(21) a. A specifier is an adjunct (Kayne (199[4]): 17).
   b. There can at most be one adjunct/specifier per phrase (Kayne (199[4]): 22).
   c. At most one head can adjoin to another head (Kayne (199[4]): 20ff).
   d. No non-head can adjoin to a head (Kayne (199[4]): 19).
   e. Adjuncts/Specifiers c-command out of the category they are adjoined to (Kayne (199[4]): 18).
   f. An X′ (the sister node of a specifier) cannot be moved (Kayne (199[4]): 17).

Interestingly, Cinque also notes that the requirement

that a head cannot be a specifier is also derived, albeit via a further assumption ("that the highest element of a chain of heads must have a specifier" (Kayne (199[4]): 31)). If a head, in order to be licensed, needs to project (and discharge its θ-role(s)), it follows that the source of a head in specifier position must be a lower head position. But then the possibility arises of excluding its moving to a specifier position as a violation of Relativized Minimality (Rizzi (1990); or "Shortest Movement"—Chomsky (1995)). A closer potential landing site (the head of the phrase it adjoins to) is skipped (this still does not prevent a head from becoming its own specifier). (Cinque 1996, 449, fn. 6)[9]

In fact, the LCA allows only a single type of constituent, as shown in (22).

(22)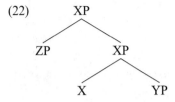

The only difference with respect to the standard X-bar theory representation is that here there is no intermediate projection (X'), since adjuncts and specifiers are not distinct.[10] All in all, the autonomous X-bar module's set of instructions has been traced to a single axiom.

It is well worth highlighting Kayne's important remark regarding the system of grammar as a whole. Where does the LCA apply? "Since I see no ... compelling evidence to the contrary," Kayne writes, "I conclude that the LCA does underlie the entire set of syntactic representations and therefore that every syntactic representation is automatically associated with a fixed linear ordering of its terminal symbols" (1994, 49). In other words, Kayne considers the LCA as a pervasive condition on syntactic representations, which is so far indirectly motivated. Whether or not this view is empirically adequate is the topic of the next section and will constitute the central issue of this work.

To summarize the situation so far: A tree embodies two distinct dimensions: hierarchical and linear. It has been standardly assumed that the two dimensions are independent—that is, that any given hierarchy can be associated to more than one linear order. The LCA proposes that the two dimensions are interlocked. More specifically, according to the LCA the property of antisymmetry inherent in precedence is inherited by the hierarchical structure. Technically, this is implemented by assuming that the locally linear order of asymmetric c-command defined on nonterminal nodes is mapped in a unique way into precedence on terminal nodes. The LCA requires the result of mapping to be a linear order itself. This theory has far-reaching and pervasive consequences for syntax, in both theoretical and comparative terms. We have concentrated on one specific consequence: from the LCA, the fundamental theorem follows that a well-formed tree may not contain two nonterminal nodes symmetrically c-commanding each other unless at most one of the two nonterminal nodes contains (at least) another nonterminal node. If this were not so, then the (sets of) terminal nodes dominated by the two symmetric nodes would not be linearly ordered—an offending configuration termed here a "point of symmetry." Finally, the LCA has been assumed to apply pervasively, at all levels of representation, and the central topic of this book —whether this assumption is empirically correct—has been addressed.

2.2 The Role of Empty Categories in Linearization: Dynamic Antisymmetry

The LCA maps hierarchy into linear order at all levels of representation. That linguistic structures are linear at some point is an obvious effect of the (human) communication system. The articulatory-perceptual performance system parses signals that evolve in time; necessarily, then, the grammatical relations that are established within the complex bidimensional architecture of phrases must be "flattened" and words must be arranged into sequences. If we take minimalism seriously, the best of all possible universal grammars would be more parsimonious: linearization would be an interface phenomenon, the relevant interface level obviously being PF.

The central intent of this book is to push this reasoning to the limit and propose that the LCA, mapping hierarchy onto linear order, is active only when linear order is required by definition—that is, only when words are spelled out. To implement this proposal, I will adopt a weak version of the antisymmetry of syntax, assuming that points of symmetry are tolerated before linearization is required. Intuitively, the guiding idea is to link movement to the geometry of phrase structure in the sense that movement rescues those structures that contain a point of symmetry. In other words, I will explore the following informal conjecture:

(23) Movement is driven by the search for antisymmetry.

Why, in principle, can movement solve the problem posed by the presence of points of symmetry in the syntactic tree? Simply put, the idea is that the LCA cannot tolerate a point of symmetry because such a point precludes fixing the linear order of terminal nodes included in it at PF. By definition, traces are not visible in the linear sequence at PF. Thus, if one of the elements constituting the point of symmetry is a trace, no problem is expected to arise; technically, let us say that movement *neutralizes* a point of symmetry.[11] Since this theory links (weak) antisymmetry with the theory of movement, I will call it *Dynamic Antisymmetry*.

Before illustrating how the theory works, I would like to make two general remarks. First, if this proposal proves empirically adequate, one major consequence will be that movement will not be considered as "motivated by interpretive requirements that are externally imposed by our systems of thought, which have these special properties, so the study of language use indicates" (Chomsky 1998). In fact, movement will be a blind mechanism, an automatic by-product of the process of linearization. The "task" of movement will be simply that of rescuing those structures that would fail to be linearized at PF. I will come back to these reflections in chapter 4.

Second, the hypothesis in (23) is a powerful one—indeed, too powerful for all of its consequences to be checked in a single work. Movement involves many heterogeneous domains of grammar, many of them still being debated from different points of view (head movement being one case; see, e.g., Chomsky 1999, 2000, Kayne 1999, Brody 1999). My limited goal here is to suggest that such a hypothesis offers a different perspective on two central aspects of the syntax of natural language, movement and phrase structure, suggesting specifically that movement is derivative from phrase structure. As usual, only empirical inquiry can decide. Let us now start to explore some representative cases.

Chapter 3

Sources of Symmetry

My goal in this chapter is to show how a Dynamic Asymmetry theory of movement works. This is of course not an exhaustive treatise on movement. Movement is involved in virtually all grammatical constructions, and I will not attempt to rebuild all domains accordingly. Instead, I will approach the issue in a different way, by taking two conceptually different paths: on the one hand, I will argue against the current theory of movement based on checking of uninterpretable features; on the other, I will indicate the general design of grammar that Dynamic Antisymmetry points to, on the basis of selected empirical cases.

3.1   The Typology of Symmetry

From a categorial point of view, we expect there to be only two types of points of symmetry: between two maximal projections (XP) or between two heads (X^0). A head X^0 and a maximal projection XP cannot constitute because the two nonterminal nodes immediately dominating the two terminal nodes do not c-command each other. From a structural point of view, however, there can be more than two types, depending on the way the two maximal projections are merged.[1] In fact, a preliminary theoretical question arises here: how many types of points of symmetry can be generated in principle? Before addressing this issue, I will anticipate the results somewhat as a guideline. Recall that antisymmetry allows only two types of syntactic constituents, heads (X^0) and nonheads (XP); intermediate projections are not admissible. As a first approximation, then, at least three types of points of symmetry are possible, since maximal projections can form two distinct constructions that constitute a point of symmetry. The three types, including "head-head" constructions, can be represented as in (1).

(1) a.

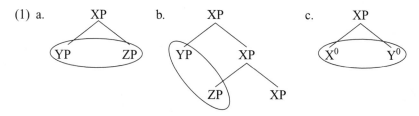

Three typical syntactic configurations are easily recognized here: small clauses (1a), multiple-spec constructions (1b), and clitic complementation (1c). In this chapter we will explore instances of each; the guiding hypothesis will be that movement can be traced to these three configurations. Notice that in each case the LCA is violated. Recall that a well-formed tree[2] cannot contain two nonterminal nodes symmetrically c-commanding each other unless at most one of the two nonterminal nodes contains (at least) another nonterminal node. If this requirement is not met, the terminal nodes fail to linearize. Thus, (1) illustrates the three basic potential offending cases for the LCA and the trigger for movement.[3]

The question now is whether these structures can be generated. This question is not trivial, and it involves commitment on the way a necessary syntactic operation works, namely, Merge. Let us first adopt an intuitive notion of Merge: Merge simply takes two syntactic objects and yields a single object. A priori, (1b) and (1c) are unproblematic; leaving aside the empirical questions posed by multiple-spec constructions, Merge can certainly generate these two structures. In particular, (1b) is adjunction to a maximal projection and (1c) is merger of a head with a head.[4] This is not to say that (1b) and (1c) must necessarily correspond to real syntactic objects. There could perhaps be independent reasons to avoid them (say, based on θ-theory), but there is no reason why Merge cannot construct them. On the other hand, (1a) appears to be anomalous: two distinct maximal projections are merged to yield a third distinct maximal projection. This is not immediately compatible with the current interpretation of Merge (see Chomsky 1995, 2000). Thus, preliminarily we need to focus on this very notion.

Merge is a basic syntactic operation that takes two distinct constituents α and β as input and gives a larger constituent K as output. What are the possible labels for K? Order being irrelevant, the standard view is that there are only two options. These can be represented as follows, using the format given by Chomsky (1995, 243–248):

(2) $\forall$ α, β, Merge yields K:
   a. K = {α, {α, β}}
   b. K = {$\langle \alpha, \alpha \rangle$, {$\alpha, \beta$}}

This formalism is to be read as follows. The elements contained in the embedded braces are the immediate constituents of the phrase; the residue is the label of the phrase itself. As suggested by the labeling, the essential property of Merge is that it is "minimal," in that the resulting constituent is formed without adding extra information with respect to α and β themselves. It can be either a simple label (either α or β; i.e., substitution as in (2a)) or a complex label (made by the ordered pair of the projecting element, here $\langle \alpha, \alpha \rangle$; i.e., adjunction as in (2b)); "[a]djunction differs from substitution, then, only in that it forms a two-segment category rather than a new category" (Chomsky 1995, 248). Again, what is crucial in both cases is that Merge does not add extra information. Notice that the way Merge is defined here assigns it a further conceptually distinct property: not only are constituents formed without adding extra information with respect to α and β themselves, but the output is entirely made up of the information associated with one item or the other. In other words, the way Merge is defined in (2) implies that there are no "mixed" labels—say, γ—made by composing hybrid information from the two items; Merge is an asymmetric operation.

Now, the way Merge is defined here leaves open a third option that is fully compatible with Merge's essential property of not adding extra information with respect to α and β and with the idea that there are no mixed labels γ. Specifically, there is another possible output of Merge that (2) does not consider: one where neither α nor β projects. Strictly speaking, in such a case one could still maintain that Merge is minimal in that it does not add extra information and in that there are no mixed labels. The question is, are there any empirical reasons to assume this third option?

I would like to suggest that such a "neutral" combination—merging two items without projecting either one—has a natural empirical correlate in the construction known as *small clauses*. Since they were first hypothesized to be syntactic units (see Williams 1975), the identification of small clauses has engendered lively debate. In fact, researchers have suggested that they are found in many contexts: for example, as reduced relative clauses, as in [sc *the man driving the bus*] (as in Williams's original proposal); as complements of *believe*-type verbs, as in *Mary considers* [sc *John the cause*] (Chomsky 1981); in double object constructions, as in *John gave* [sc *Mary a book*] (Kayne 1984); in raising-verb contexts, as in

John is [sc *t a fool*], *John seems* [sc *t a fool*], *The cause of the riot is* [sc *John t*], *It seems* [sc *[that John is a fool] t*] (Stowell 1981, Burzio 1986, Moro 1997b, and references cited there); in existential sentences, as in *There is* [sc *a fool in the garden*] (Williams 1984, Stowell 1981, Burzio 1986) and as in *There is* [sc *a problem t*] (Moro 1997b); in adjunct constructions, as in *John left the room* [sc *PRO angry*] (Williams 1980, Chomsky 1981); in perceptual reports, as in *Maria vide* [sc *Gianni che correva*] 'lit. Maria saw Gianni that was running' (Cinque 1995); in colloquial expressions, as in [sc *Me angry?*] (Haegeman 1990); in unaccusatives, as in *There arrived* [sc *a man t*] (Moro 1990, 1997b); and in possessive constructions, as in *Gianni c'ha* [sc *un gatto t*] 'lit. Gianni there-has a cat' (Moro 1997b). Of course, I cannot address this issue in full; nevertheless, a brief survey of research on small clauses will highlight the relevance of this construction to the theoretical issue posed by Merge.

A long-standing question concerning small clauses is how to capture the facts that (unlike full clauses) they seem not to be projected by an inflectional head (hence the label *small*) and that their distribution differs from that of their components (e.g., the distribution of *the cage empty* differs from that of *the cage* and of *empty*). Moreover, the latter fact has a semantic counterpart that is too special to be accidental. A small clause is made by connecting a subject and a predicate, but the resulting constituent has a totally different grammatical status. It is neither a subject nor a predicate: it is a (small) clause.[5] This twofold nature of small clauses has been captured in different ways. The development of research on small clauses directly reflects the effort to resolve the tension between the observed facts.

Originally, the small clause constituent was represented with an autonomous label (i.e., *SC*), immediately connecting two maximal projections (e.g., [DP *the cage*] and [AP *empty*]) (see Williams 1975).

(3)   SC

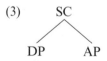

Several attempts have been made to refine this representation. At least two lines of research can be distinguished: one that aims at regularizing the structure of the small clause with respect to X-bar theory by identifying a functional head that projects it (see, e.g., Kayne 1985, Moro 1988, Bowers 1993), and one that aims at reducing small clauses to cases of adjunction to the predicate (see, e.g., Stowell 1981, Manzini 1983, Longobardi 1988).

An example of the former line of research is Moro 1988, where the complement of the copula, a prototypical instance of a small clause, is analyzed as an AgrP (and the copula as a T^0).[6]

(4)

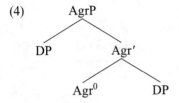

Such a more articulated structure was motivated by certain properties of copular constructions that I leave aside here. The observation that deserves highlighting is that if we adopt this representation, the link between the subject and the predicate is performed by Agr^0. I also observed that although this representation solves many problems, certain empirical data run counter to it. In what follows I will outline those considerations.

Let us consider Italian, whose rich morphology will help in the exposition of the argument. Consider two DPs, differing in both gender and number.

(5) a. [DP questi   libri]
         there.MASC.PL books.MASC.PL
    b. [DP la   causa   della rivolta]
         the.FEM.SG cause.FEM.SG of-the riot

These two DPs can enter into a predicative relation, yielding a perfectly well formed nominal small clause. If a small clause is an AgrP, then we expect the two DPs playing the role of subject and predicate to agree. Let us look at the data:

(6) Gianni ritiene   [SC[DP questi libri] [DP la causa della rivolta]].
     Gianni considers   these books   the cause of-the riot

Clearly, there is no agreement at all, not even number agreement. The two DPs enter into a predicative relation without matching any component of their φ-features. Of course, this is not to say that agreement is impossible in Italian nominal small clauses. In cases like the following, it is in fact obligatory:

(7) a.   Gianni ritiene   [SC[DP queste ragazze] [DP le   sue   migliori
          Gianni considers   these girls   the.PL his.PL best.PL
          amiche]].
          friends.PL

b. *Gianni ritiene   [SC[DP queste ragazze [DP la   sua   migliore
   Gianni considers   these   girls   the.SG his.SG best.SG
   amica]].
   friend.SG

We can leave aside the explanation for this important difference (see, e.g., Higginbotham 1983, 1990, and references cited there). What interests us here is the very fact that there is at least one case where the subject and the predicate need not agree. We can reasonably take this case to be a sufficient reason to infer that predication need not necessarily be mediated by agreement between the subject and the predicate. In fact, a cursory crosslinguistic survey largely confirms this assumption. A classic case is provided by German data.

(8) a. Das Haus ist neu.
       the house is new.NULL AGR
    b. Das neue   Haus
       the new.NEUT.SG house

The conclusion is clear: the adjective agrees with the noun only when it does not play the role of a (clausal) predicate.[7]

In sum, although the predicative relation may involve a form of agreement, agreement cannot be a necessary condition for establishing this relation. In other words, from the very fact that among nominal small clauses we find an instance of predication without agreement, we can conclude that small clauses need not necessarily be analyzed as AgrPs.[8] Small clauses may display subject-predicate agreement, as in the case of AP predicates, but this should be regarded as an independent fact that has nothing to do with predication. Rather, agreement depends on the specific morphological necessities of the predicate in a given language. In other words, there are no reasons to analyze small clauses (uniformly) as projections of Agr^0 heads.

Along with these empirical arguments, Chomsky (1995) has suggested that small clauses should not be analyzed as AgrPs for theoretical reasons. This proposal is part of a broader project to avoid recourse to Agr^{0}s in general, going back to the theory that preceded the so-called split-Infl hypothesis. In fact, Chomsky's specific proposal concerning small clauses is to go back to "something like the original assumptions of Stowell (1978)" (Chomsky 1995, 354). What are those original assumptions? The formal solution Stowell proposed is particularly revealing with respect to the problem discussed here. On the one hand, Stowell proposed that small clauses are in fact the result of bare adjunction; on the other, the necessity

of signaling the special status of this adjunct construction led him to mark
it with a special diacritic (an asterisk). So a small clause like *the cage
empty* would be represented as in (9).

(9)   *AP

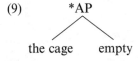

   the cage   empty

Clearly, Merge as stated in (2) cannot immediately capture this special
instance of adjunction. Take α and β to be the subject and the predicative
noun phrase of the small clause in (9): respectively, *the cage* and *empty*.
The first option, (2a), is to be excluded because we do not want the
resulting constituent to be either α or β; that is, the small clause must not
have the same distribution as either of its parts. The second option, (2b),
is also problematic. In fact, it reproduces the same problems that Stowell
solved in the 1970s framework by adding an asterisk to the final segment
of the larger category in (9): we want to be able to distinguish between
adjunction and small clauses. Of course, in a minimalist framework
adopting some version of Merge, recourse to an asterisk is impossible; it
would be an ad hoc notational solution.

The third option for Merge, suggested above, offers a possible solution
to this puzzle. Merge allows generation of underspecified (i.e., unlabeled)
constituents. These constituents can now be associated to this special case
of adjunction. More explicitly, I propose that all and only small clauses
(and their interpretive correlate, predicative linking) be associated to these
unlabeled constituents. In the next section I will offer empirical evidence
to support this analysis and to distinguish among different types of small
clauses. I will show that there is need to distinguish at least two types of
what are now labeled simply "small clauses": *bare* small clauses, which
are complements of the copula, and *rich* small clauses, which are complements of *believe*-type verbs. For now, though, let us just assume that
there are good reasons, both empirical and theoretical, to assume that
Merge can generate a "flat" constituent like the one in (1a). Still, the
problem arises of how this process can be formally captured within the
framework adopted in (2). Strictly speaking, this does not undermine
the argument. In fact, the essential idea we want to adopt should be
intuitively clear. For any given unordered pair α and β, we want Merge to
be able to yield two distinct types of output: it can either asymmetrically
project either α or β (in complement and adjunct structures) or not project
at all (in small clause structures). In both cases, again, the essential properties of Merge are preserved: first, the output does not add extra infor-

mation; second, the output contains no mixed labels. However, one could also try to implement this idea within the formalism in (2). One possibility would be to add (c) to it, as in (10).

(10) $\forall \alpha, \beta$, Merge yields K:
  a. $K = \{\alpha, \{\alpha, \beta\}\}$
  b. $K = \{\langle \alpha, \alpha \rangle, \{\alpha, \beta\}\}$
  c. $K = \{\langle \emptyset \rangle, \{\alpha, \beta\}\}$

The small clause (and its interpretive correlate, predicative linking) would then be just this: the result of merging α and β when neither projects. It is not substitution, as in Stowell's original proposal, but it is also not "pure" adjunction, where the resulting label is the ordered pair of features of the projecting element. This is compatible with the essential properties of Merge. In fact, it seems to capture an intuitive property of predication: neither the subject nor the predicate prevails.[9] As for the correlation of small clauses with predicative linking, we will come back to this issue later. Notice that the idea that the absence of projection correlates with predication has the welcome result of excluding small clauses that do not contain a possible subject (a noun phrase or a clause). In other words, it excludes small clauses for example of the type *AP AP, *AP PP, or *PP PP, in which no argument (to predicate something of) is available. All in all, we will assume that a small clause is to be represented much in the original sense as the result of merging two maximal projections (a subject and a predicate), where neither one projects and no head intervenes.

With this in mind, let us consider the three structures in (1); we will find that they are all (and the only)[10] points of symmetry. Let us start with the small clause type, (1a). This structure includes two nonterminals (YP and ZP) that c-command each other and that contain at least another nonterminal (Y^0 and its complement QP, Z^0 and its complement RP); the nonterminals projecting YP and ZP, then, would prevent the tree from linearizing. For the sake of clarity, I represent the situation in greater detail in (11) by indicating the terminals dominated by the head of YP (y) and by the head of ZP (z).

(11)

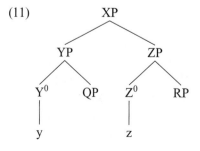

Notice that ZP c-commands Y^0 but Y^0 does not c-command ZP; thus, the terminals dominated by ZP, including z, precede the terminal dominated by Y^0, namely, y (i.e., z precedes y). On the other hand, YP c-commands Z^0 but Z^0 does not c-command YP; thus, the terminals dominated by YP, including y, precede the terminals dominated by Z^0, namely, z, (i.e., y precedes z). All in all, (11) violates the LCA, since it is the case both that z precedes y and that y precedes z; that is, d(A) is not a linear ordering since it includes both $\langle z, y \rangle$ and $\langle y, z \rangle$.

The same reasoning can be applied to (1b), the case of multiple-spec constructions. In fact, modulo the number of segments of XP, the proper metric given by c-command makes YP and ZP c-command each other, yielding the same result as in (11); recall that only categories can c-command (and be c-commanded) and that for a category α to c-command a category β, no segment of α can dominate β. Thus, in (1b) both YP and ZP c-command out of XP and then c-command each other, constituting a point of symmetry, exactly as YP and ZP do in (11).

Case (1c) differs from the two we have just looked at. In (1c) the two nonterminals c-command each other; that is, X^0 and Y^0 each immediately dominate a terminal (x and y, respectively).

(12)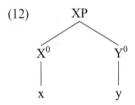

In this case no nonterminal asymmetrically c-commands another; thus, there is no pair that can linearize x and y. To put it more formally, since A is empty, d(A) is also empty. For a different reason than (1a) and (1b), then, (1c) violates the LCA.

The aim of this chapter is to show that the three abstract structures in (1) are empirically relevant in that they can be considered triggers for movement. In fact, according to Dynamic Antisymmetry these structures can be generated provided that movement rescues them at Spell-Out, where linear order is required. Movement turns one of the two "poles" of the point of symmetry into an empty category (t) and thereby neutralizes the problem posed by linearization.

The threefold partition in (1) serves as an organizing principle for the empirical data examined in this chapter. Section 3.2 discusses small clauses as in (1a) as triggers for movement, distinguishing between complements of the copula and complements of *believe*-type verbs and exploring some peculiar types of *wh*-movement involving splitting (e.g., the German *was-für* split cases). Section 3.3 studies *do*-support and rightward agreement in Italian from a Dynamic Asymmetry point of view, showing that these phenomena can be analyzed as instances of multiple-spec constructions as in (1b). Finally, section 3.4 approaches aspects of cliticization phenomena in Italian from a Dynamic Asymmetry perspective, showing that they can be interpreted as instances of the structure in (1c).

3.2   Bare Small Clauses

Let us concentrate on small clauses. As noted earlier, the status of this grammatical structure has been controversial since it was first proposed by Williams (1975). In general, a small clause is considered to be a constituent in which two phrasal categories are connected by a predicative relation; however, it has also been proposed that small clauses are not essentially related to predication (see Kayne 1984). (I will not go into this debate here; for detailed discussion, see Cardinaletti and Guasti 1995, Graffi 1997, and references cited there.) First I will analyze two typical constructions containing small clauses—copular sentences and sentences with *believe*-type verbs—and refine the analysis by distinguishing two types of small clauses (section 3.2.1); then I will propose that a small clause construction is also involved in certain instances of *wh*-movement (section 3.2.2).

3.2.1   Copular Sentences versus *Believe*-Type Verbs

In chapter 1 we considered the analysis of simple transitive sentences of the type *DP V DP* in the minimalist framework. In this framework movement is regarded as a way to delete uninterpretable features—a prototypical example being Case features. Beginning with a simple example like (13), let us concentrate on nominative Case features associated with the subject of a tensed clause.

(13) John has always read books.

Following usual assumptions, we take the subject to be generated inside VP (more specifically in the specifier position of *v*P, if one adopts a Larsonian shell analysis of transitive verb phrases; see Chomsky 1995, 352).

The subject has a nominative Case feature associated with it; this feature is abstract here but could be overtly realized in English if the subject were a pronoun, namely, *he*. (Nominative) Case features are uninterpretable; therefore, they must be erased. The system forces the subject to move to the specifier position of the inflectional system (specifier of IP, in a syncretic analysis), crossing over the adverb and the auxiliary. In such a position the uninterpretable nominative Case feature is deleted. Now, as noted earlier, there are different ways to implement such a process; in previous systems the features contained in the noun phrase, including Case features, could be directly attracted to the higher position (Chomsky 1993, 1995).[11] In more recent proposals Case is not directly visible to the operation yielding movement; nevertheless, other devices (e.g., the so-called EPP-features; see Chomsky 2000, 122, also Chomsky 1999) force the noun phrase to move and then to delete Case. Whether Case is directly or indirectly involved in triggering movement, the result is the same: the noun phrase containing the uninterpretable Case feature is moved to a specifier position where such uninterpretable features are deleted.

Similar considerations hold in general for structural Case. However, for present purposes it is not necessary to discuss all types of Case. Instead, I would simply like to show that the system based on the hypothesis that movement is required to delete uninterpretable features is not workable. To do so, I will consider a particular type of *DP V DP* sentence, namely, sentences where V is the copula. I will adopt the unified theory of copular constructions presented in previous works of mine (Moro 1988, 1997b; see the appendix for a synthetic illustration of this theory). Consider the following two sentences:

(14) a. John is the cause of the riot.
     b. The cause of the riot is John.

Although these sentences contain the same lexical elements, they differ in many respects. All the differences can be captured by assuming that whereas in (14a) the subject *John* is raised to preverbal position and the predicative noun phrase *the cause of the riot* is left in situ in the small clause, in (14b) the subject *John* is left in situ in the small clause and the predicative noun phrase *the cause of the riot* is raised to preverbal position. These two basic types have been called *canonical* and *inverse* copular constructions, respectively. Adopting a very simplified labeling, we can represent these two types as in (15).[12]

(15) a.   IP   (canonical)

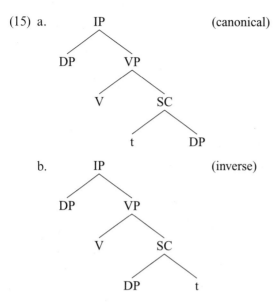

b.   IP   (inverse)

What is relevant here is that in the inverse construction the subject stays in situ in the small clause. As is the case for all subjects (of tensed clauses), we assume the null hypothesis, namely, that the subject of a(n inverse) copular construction is assigned nominative Case features. That this hypothesis is correct can be shown by using pronouns. Italian provides particularly clear examples. A pronominal equivalent of the inverse structure in (14b) is (16), where the pronoun in subject position is indeed nominative: the nominative first person singular pronoun *io*.

(16) La causa della   rivolta sono io t.
     the cause of-the riot   am   I

This is sufficient for our purposes: inverse copular constructions provide a good test for evaluating the adequacy of the theory of movement based on the necessity of deleting uninterpretable features (regarding verbal agreement, see section 3.3.2).

   The situation is as follows: the postverbal subject in (16) (or equivalently its structural small clause correlate in (15b)) should move covertly to delete the uninterpretable nominative Case features associated with it. (Recall that Case is always uninterpretable, whatever item it is associated with). This consequence is empirically incorrect. In fact, it runs counter to the major empirical generalization resulting from the analysis of copular constructions, namely, that the subject of an inverse copular sentence is completely opaque to movement, both overt and covert: it cannot be moved as a whole and extraction cannot take place from it (for the empirical reasons, see the appendix). Moreover, it is important to notice that we cannot consistently appeal to the alternative operation Agree here. As noted in section 1.3.1, "... Merge or Agree (or their combination) preempts Move, which is a 'last resort,' chosen when nothing else is possible" (Chomsky 2000, 102). Thus, if Agree could delete the uninterpretable (Case) features of the subject of an inverse copular sentence, we would predict that it should never move—a prediction that is plainly false given that the lexical entries yielding (16) are exactly the same as those yielding the canonical counterpart where the subject does move (*io sono t la causa della rivolta*), crucially including *pro* (see (83) in section 3.3.2).[13]

The problem is clear. On the one hand, covert movement cannot take place because there is overwhelming evidence that the subject of an inverse copular sentence never moves (either overtly or covertly). On the other, Agree cannot plausibly apply; if it did, the subject should never move to delete its uninterpretable features, a prediction that is plainly false in view of canonical copular sentences. This conflict is a serious problem for the theory that movement takes place for morphological reasons. Perhaps there are ways to adjust the theory to fit these examples; however, I will not attempt to discover them. Rather, I will offer an alternative, natural account based on Dynamic Antisymmetry. In fact, Dynamic Antisymmetry can immediately explain raising out of the small clause. Simply put, the small clause constitutes a point of symmetry and this is what triggers movement. The small clause structure violates the LCA, making linearization of the associated terminal nodes impossible; movement rescues the structure by "neutralizing" one pole of the point of symmetry, that is, by turning it into an empty category (*t*). Clearly, the problems related to the morphological theory of movement do not arise here. More specifically, there is no need to justify covert movement of the residual noun phrase in the small clause; once either noun phrase constituting the small clause is removed, the structure is fully compatible with the LCA because the point of symmetry is neutralized.

However, this solution based on Dynamic Antisymmetry does pose a potential problem that must be solved. Consider the following sentence in Italian:

(17) Gianni ritiene [α queste foto   la causa della rivolta].
     Gianni considers these   pictures the cause of-the riot

The complement of *ritiene*, a prototypical *believe*-type verb, has been generally considered a small clause constituent on a par with the complement of the copula. If the two constituents were identical, sentences like (17) would be major counterexamples to a Dynamic Antisymmetry account: one of the two noun phrases should have moved overtly out of the small clause to neutralize the point of symmetry, contrary to fact. Indeed, a Dynamic Antisymmetry approach would force us to assume that the complement of a *believe*-type verb is richer—more articulated in structure—than the complement of the copula. That this is correct needs to be proved on empirical grounds. We will look at three types of evidence, from the realms of adverbs, predicative markers, and cliticization phenomena.

Let us begin with adverbs. We know that adverbs like Italian *in alcun modo* 'in any way', which are polarity items, are licensed in the specifier position of a functional head—say, F^0.[14]

(18) ... [$_{FP}$[in alcun modo] F^0 ...
               in any   way
         'by no means'

Let us start by assuming that the complement of a *believe*-type verb is indeed a small clause. Adverbial elements like the one in (18) can occur between the subject and the predicate of a small clause like the one in (17).

(19) Gianni non ritiene   [queste foto   [in alcun modo] la   causa
     Gianni not considers these pictures in any   way   the cause
     della   rivolta].
     of-the riot

This suggests that the structure that is the complement of the *believe*-type verb is not a "bare" small clause like the small clauses found in copular sentences, but a richer construction involving at least one functional projection. Let us now try the adverbial test with copular constructions: if the adverbial element cannot appear in the small clause complement of the copula, then we will not be able to distinguish the two cases and (17) really will be a counterexample to Dynamic Antisymmetry. Consider a canonical copular structure first (see (15a)).

(20) Gianni non è in alcun modo la   causa della   rivolta.
     Gianni not is in any   way   the cause of-the riot

The adverbial phrase *in alcun modo* can indeed also appear in the canonical copular sentence, but this tells us very little. In particular, since the subject has been raised from within the small clause, we cannot decide between the structural representations in (21a) and (21b).

(21) a. Gianni non è in alcun modo [$_{SC}$ t la causa della rivolta].
     b. Gianni non è [$_{SC}$ t in alcun modo la causa della rivolta].

The subject of the small clause signals the left boundary of the clause; displacing it makes the diagnostic impossible. Inverse copular sentences are much more revealing. In this type of structure we know that the subject cannot be displaced; thus, its position marks the left boundary of the small clause. If the adverbial element can appear after it, then the small clause complement of the copula must be as rich in structure as the small clause complement of *believe*-type verbs. This is the result of the test:

(22) a. La causa della   rivolta non è in alcun modo [$_{SC}$ Gianni t].
         the causa of-the riot   not is in any way   Gianni
     b. *La causa della   rivolta non è [$_{SC}$ Gianni in alcun modo t].
         the cause of-the riot   not is   Gianni in any   way

Clearly, the adverbial phrase must precede the subject of the small clause, unlike in the case of *believe*-type verbs.[15] This fact suggests that there are good reasons to assume that the complement of the copula does not contain functional projections that could host the subject, unlike the complement of a *believe*-type verb. Synthetically, we can conclude that only the copula has a small clause complement in the specific sense adopted here (call it a *bare* small clause). Sentence (17) involving a *believe*-type verb instead receives the following simplified representation, where the complement of the verb (here labeled as an undefined functional projection, FP) is a much richer constituent:

(23) Gianni non ritiene   [$_{FP}$ queste foto F^0 ... in alcun modo F^0 ...
     Gianni not considers   these   pictures   in any
     [$_{SC}$ la   causa ...
          the cause

All in all, this means that (17) is not a counterexample to Dynamic Antisymmetry. The clausal complement of a *believe*-type verb is a richer constituent that does not require movement because it does not contain points of symmetry (at the FP level).[16]

A second argument in favor of the hypothesis that the complement of a *believe*-type verb is richer than the complement of the copula comes from the distribution of predicative markers such as Italian *come* and English *as*. It has been proposed that the complement of *believe*-type verbs is generated by (abstract) heads that instantiate the predicative relation (see, e.g., Moro 1988, Bowers 1993). The proposal is based on the fact that the subject and the predicate can be separated by elements like Italian *come* and English *as* (or their crosslinguistic equivalents). For example:

(24) Maria considera [Gianni (come) il   colpevole].
        Maria considers Gianni as   the culprit

The null hypothesis is that *come* 'as' is the overt realization of the functional head projecting the clausal constituent. Now, it seems that if it is tenable, this argument holds only for the "richer" type of small clause, namely, the complement of *believe*-type verbs. This is easily shown to be true: *come* cannot occur in copular sentences like (25), unless it is interpreted as a predicate itself ('similar to', 'like').

(25) Gianni è (*come) il   colpevole.
        Gianni is as   the culprit

Again, if the constituents following the copula and a *believe*-type verb were structurally identical, the contrast could not be captured; instead, it seems reasonable to assume that *come* overtly marks the head projecting the embedded clausal constituent. All in all, the complement of *believe*-type verbs appears to be richer than the bare small clause complement of the copula.

A third argument comes from cliticization. In Italian a predicative noun phrase can be cliticized by means of the uninflected clitic *lo*.

(26) a. Queste foto   sono la causa della rivolta.
           these   pictures are the cause of-the riot
       b. Queste foto   lo sono t.
           these   pictures LO are

It is also well known that the same process is blocked for predicative noun phrases in the complement of *believe*-type verbs in both active and passive constructions (see Burzio 1986 for references and discussion).

(27) a. Gianni ritiene   queste foto   la causa della rivolta.
           Gianni considers these   pictures the cause of-the riot
       b. *Gianni lo ritiene   queste foto   t.
           Gianni LO considers these   pictures
       c. *Queste foto   lo sono ritenute   t t.
           these   pictures LO are   considered

The richer structure independently adduced to account for the distribution of adverbs and predicative markers in the complement of *believe*-type verbs can now be exploited to account for the contrast between (26b) and (27b). Let us focus on the two structures:

(28) a. Queste foto   lo sono [t t].
         these   photos LO are
     b. *Gianni lo ritiene   [queste foto F^0 ... t]
         Gianni LO considers these   pictures

In fact, the contrast can now be reduced to a Relativized Minimality effect: we know that clitics move as maximal projections in the intermediate steps of movement (see Kayne 1989 and references cited there). This is shown by agreement along the clitic's path.

(29) a. Gianni ha voluto   vedere due ragazze.
         Gianni has wanted.NEUT see.INF two girls
     b. Gianni le   ha t volute   vedere t.
         Gianni them.FEM has   wanted.FEM see.INF

Thus, it is not unreasonable to assume that in (28b) the chain of the clitic violates Relativized Minimality because the clitic does not pass through the intermediate potential landing site. Notice that clitic movement is not always impossible from the clausal constituent. For example, the subject of the clausal complement of a *believe*-type verb can undergo cliticization.

(30) Gianni le ritiene   [t la causa della   rivolta].
      Gianni them-considers   the cause of-the riot

Notice also that movement cannot take place from within the predicative noun phrase of the clausal complement of a *believe*-type verb.

(31) a. Gianni ritiene   queste sue foto   di Maria [la causa della
         Gianni considers these   his pictures of Maria the cause of-the
         rivolta].
         riot
     b. *Gianni ne   ritiene   queste sue foto   di Maria [la
         Gianni of-it considers these   his pictures of Maria the
         causa t].
         cause

This precludes the possibility that the blocking of cliticization is inherently related to the predicative status of *lo* (and the fact that it is not inflected); rather, it must be a genuine structural fact.

As it turns out, then, we have eliminated the apparent counterexample to Dynamic Antisymmetry in (17): there is no need for either noun phrase in the complement of a *believe*-type verb to be moved (across the verb), because a complement of a *believe*-type verb does not constitute a point of symmetry. The theory has forced us to assume that the small clause complement of this type of verb is richer in structure than the bare small clause complement of the copula, and the facts support the theory. Crucially, unlike what we find with copular sentences, the complement of *believe*-type verbs includes at least one functional head that prevents the creation of a point of symmetry.

So far, then, Dynamic Antisymmetry appears to be empirically more adequate than the morphological theory of movement (movement as a way to delete uninterpretable features). Unlike the morphological theory, for which inverse copular sentences pose a problem, Dynamic Antisymmetry offers a natural explanation for raising in both canonical and inverse copular sentences. There is no need to go against the well-established generalization that the subject of inverse copular sentences never moves, in order to justify nominative Case feature deletion; simply, once the predicate has been raised, there is no need to covertly move any constituent further. The point of symmetry is already neutralized.

Before we examine a second instance of the same type of point of symmetry (small clauses), a methodological issue must be addressed. Suppose we admit that the case study illustrated here is a genuine counterexample to the morphological theory of movement. What is the relevance of a single anomalous case for the theory in general? Two lines of reasoning are possible. First, one could take a single counterexample as a reason for abandoning a theory as a whole. This is generally considered not a necessary move in empirical sciences; in fact, it is considered a dubious move. An irreducible phenomenon does not necessarily undermine a theory: provisorily, a theory might well tolerate a certain number of exceptions if the number of facts it explains is significant. Further developments will say whether the exceptions are genuine problems that make the theory unacceptable or whether they can be absorbed provided minor adjustments are made. In fact, there is no general rule for deciding; scientists are left to their intuition. Mathematics is totally different: there is no "quantitative" evaluation, and even a single counterexample can undermine a theory. This represents a second possible reaction to the discovery of an anomaly, which of course is not viable for linguistics. Thus, inverse copular constructions do not necessarily refute the morphological theory of movement. Indeed, one possibility would be to say they are exceptions, and to maintain the morphological theory of movement. Simply, I will not pursue this line of reasoning; instead, I assume that there are good empirical reasons to generalize the alternative proposal based on a weak version of antisymmetry to other, possibly all, cases of movement. Indirect support for this choice is suggested in the appendix, where the pervasive presence of "inverse" constructions in syntax is illustrated synthetically.

3.2.2   *Wh*-Phrases as Predicates: Splitting versus Agreement

A second case study of a small-clause-type point of symmetry involves *wh*-movement, which I will approach in this section from a Dynamic Antisymmetry perspective. Dynamic Antisymmetry claims that movement is a symmetry-breaking phenomenon. More explicitly, according to this theory movement intervenes whenever a structure would be too symmetric to be LCA compatible. In the case of copular constructions, we have seen that symmetry results from merging two maximal projections, yielding a predicative nucleus (the bare small clause). What kind of symmetry would trigger *wh*-movement? For example, in a simple case involving a *wh*-object, such as *Which books has John read?*, what is the symmetric relation that triggers movement of *which books* from post-verbal position? A Dynamic Antisymmetry approach offers at least two potential analyses. One could explore the possibility that the *wh*-object itself constitutes a point of symmetry with some other part of the structure and is displaced to neutralize that point of symmetry. Alternatively, one could consider that the point of symmetry is internal to the *wh*-object and causes the *wh*-object as a whole to move. A priori, there seems to be no reason to exclude either option. Indeed, inspection of the typology of *wh*-movement both across and within languages suggests that the second analysis is more promising on empirical grounds. It is well known that in certain languages *wh*-movement may involve splitting between the *wh*-element and associated lexical items. A prototypical case is the so-called *was-für* split construction in German, where the *wh*-phrase can be raised alone, leaving the lexical item in situ. In fact, the German equivalent of *Which books has John read?* could be *Was hat Johann für Bücher gelesen?* 'what has Johann for books read' (colloquially, "Which books has Johann read?"). In general, these constructions have been analyzed as deviating from the more basic construction not involving *für* (i.e., *Welche Bücher hat Johann gelesen?* 'Which books has Johann read?') and as being specific to Germanic languages. However, a central argument of this section will be that splitting in *wh*-constructions is more pervasive across and within languages than usually thought—in particular, that it can be found in many constructions in Romance languages such as Italian.

In this section I would like to reconsider these splitting constructions, suggesting that they reveal the otherwise hidden symmetry-breaking nature of *wh*-movement in general. More explicitly, I will propose thinking of *wh*-movement as a way to neutralize a point of symmetry that is internal to the *wh*-phrase. Of course, this change of perspective will require finding a reason to explain why splitting can be obscured, inducing pied-piping of the whole phrase. Data will consist mainly of a fragment of the relevant cases: *wh*-movement of noun phrases. Let us consider English first.

It is standardly assumed that *wh*-elements such as *which* and *what* are generated in the left periphery of the noun phrase. As a first approximation, these elements are generated in the same structural position as (generalized) quantifiers and articles, namely, D^0 (see Abney 1987 and many related works). More specifically, they are represented as higher than the NP they occur with (possibly higher than intermediate functional projections; see Cinque 1992).

(32)

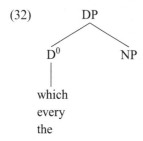

Although this assumption, which holds across languages, certainly explains many facts, there is a class of phenomena that calls for refinement. It is well known, for example, that in German and Dutch the *wh*-element and the residue of the noun phrase can be split in the so-called *was-für* and *wat-voor* constructions. Consider for example the following Dutch sentence (from Bennis 1986):

(33) Wat heeft hij voor romans geschreven?
     what has he for   novels written
     'What novels has he written?'

According to the classic analysis, the *wh*-element is extracted from the complex specifier position of the NP and the residue is left in situ, yielding the structure in (34).

(34) Wat heeft hij [NP[t voor] [N' romans]] geschreven?

Now, disregarding the obvious formal revision that Bennis's (1986) analysis in (34) should undergo, a substantial empirical problem arises: Why does this type of split involving an overt functional head affect only *wh*-elements? Can we explain it by maintaining the generalization in (32)? Perhaps more basically, what drives this type of movement? Before trying to develop a comprehensive analysis of the splitting phenomena and the reasons for movement, let us consider more empirical data.

Although this class of splitting phenomena is generally considered to be limited to the Germanic languages, an analogous phenomenon appears to occur in Italian in cases like (35a–b), which contrast with (35c–d) in that splitting is obligatory for most speakers; at a lower stylistic level (35e) is also possible, involving a particle *di*.

(35) a. Quanto sono alti?
         how   are   tall.MASC.PL
         'How tall are they?'
     b. *?Quanto alti sono?
     c. Quali   libri   hai   letto?
         which.MASC.PL books.MASC.PL have.2SG read
         'Which books have you read?'
     d. *Quali hai letto libri?
     e. Cosa/Quali   hai   letto di libri?
         what/which.MASC.PL have.2SG read of books.MASC.PL
         'Which books have you read?'

Why is this splitting process productive across and within languages, and why is it limited to *wh*-phrases? In this section I will suggest a possible refinement of (32) distinguishing *wh*-phrases from the other elements that are generated in D^0 and offer a principled reason for movement based on Dynamic Antisymmetry. This will require rethinking the role of *wh*-words like *which* by exploiting a more articulated structure of a particular type of noun phrase.

The underlying intuition I will exploit is that there is a natural association between sentences like these:

(36) a. Which books did John read?
     b. John read books of this type.

The intuition is that *which* can be regarded as the interrogative counterpart of *this type*. This is surely true from an interpretive point of view; for example, a proper answer to (36a) would be *books of this type*. My claim here is that this analogy is stronger than usually thought and that *which* is generated in a syntactic configuration similar to the one where *this type* is generated. Let us then begin by assigning a syntactic structure to (36b).[17]

The object of *read* is the complex phrase *books of this type*. This phrase is headed by *books*, and *of this type* "modifies" *books*, in a pretheoretical sense. Interestingly, this sentence can be associated with the following one:[18]

(37) John read this type of books.

Despite the superficial differences in linear order of lexical items, this sentence and (36b) are essentially synonymous, at least insofar as in both constructions *books* can be considered as the object of *read* and *this type* can be considered as modifying *books*. It would make no sense to say that *of books* is the modifier of *this type* and that the latter is the object of *read*. How can this analogy be captured? In what syntactic sense does *this type* modify *books*?

An interesting possibility, stemming from work by (among others) Kayne (1994), Den Dikken (1999), and Zamparelli (1995), is that (36b) and (37) include a clausal constituent (here, a small clause) of which *books* is the subject and *this type* is the predicate.[19]

(38) John read [... of [$_{SC}$ books this type]]

In current terms, the role of the particle *of* is claimed to be that of allowing *books* to raise to check Case in the proper configuration. Alternatively, assuming that the small clause involved here is a bare small clause of the same type as the one selected by the copula, we can simply invoke Dynamic Antisymmetry and consider movement a way to neutralize the point of symmetry constituted by the small clause.

(39) John read [books of [$_{SC}$ t this type]].

Interestingly, the parallel with copular constructions has been pursued further. The structure in (38) appears not to be the only output of the underlying form in (36b). There is a second option of raising the other DP of the small clause, directly recalling the structure of inverse copular sentences, where the subject stays in situ in the small clause and the predicate raises and crosses over it to a higher specifier position (see, e.g., Kayne 1994, 110).

(40) John read [this type of [$_{SC}$ books t]].

As usual, this proposal solves some problems and raises others.[20] On the one hand, the structures in (39) and (40) immediately capture the fact that in both cases *books* is the object of *read* and *this type* is the predicate of *books*; on the other, they lead to questions regarding Case assignment, interpretation, and many other issues. I will not pursue this analysis further here, instead assuming that it is essentially correct.

Before I apply this proposal to the analysis of *wh*-movement, I would like to address a specific problem concerning selection. An obvious requirement for this theory to succeed is that a transitive verb like *read* not select a clausal complement; if it did, it would be hard to exclude clausal complementation in different contexts and with different transitive verbs (such as *burn, copy, vaporize*). The structural definition of bare small clause and its interpretive correlate as a predicative structure (independently proposed in section 2.1) can now be exploited to solve this puzzling situation. Recall that a bare small clause is the result of merging two projections, neither of which projects further. Thus, assuming that *of* can be essentially regarded as a D^0, we can simply say that the transitive verb uniformly selects a DP. The problem of selection is now reformulated as the question of whether D^0 can take a clausal complement. In fact, this assumption is independently well founded on comparative grounds. In languages like Italian, for example, articles can take infinitival complements: *l'andare a Roma* 'the go to Rome', *uno scrivere scorrevole* 'a write smoothly', and so on. In Spanish, articles can even take full inflected CPs as complements: *Estoy contento del que tu salgas* 'am happy of-the that you leave', *El que tu leyas es natural* 'the that you read is natural' (see Donati 1995 and references cited there). All in all, then, we can assume that the verb selects a DP and that the D^0 selects a clausal constituent that is formed by merging a noun phrase with another phrase neither of which projects further.

Another question concerns the noun phrase occurring in the small clause. Apparently, only NPs can occur there, as opposed to full DPs (e.g., **this type of the books*). Two competing solutions come to mind. One possibility is that the restriction to bare NPs is imposed by D^0; that would imply that D^0 is able to affect the categorial selection of the lower subject in the small clause. Another is that the subject of the small clause is a DP and that the D^0 contained in it is deleted under identity with the higher D^0. Since this is essentially the solution independently proposed by Bianchi (2000) for relative clauses, I will adopt it as an instance of a more general strategy.

Let us now go back to the analogy between (36a) and (36b). If the interpretive analogy carries over to their syntactic structures, then a partial analysis of (36a) should include the following structure:

(41) John read ... [sc books which]

In other words, I propose that the structural representation in (42b) be adopted for *wh*-phrases in place of the one in (32) (repeated here as (42a)), which should be reserved for quantifiers.[21]

(42) a.

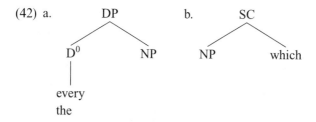

The *wh*-element *which* now occupies the same structural position as *this type* in (38), namely, that of predicative (noun phrase);[22] the generalized quantifiers *every* and *the* are generated in a different position, here represented as D^0.[23]

Let us now go back to the splitting phenomena illustrated earlier. If we adopt the alternative representation suggested here, these splitting phenomena naturally follow from Dynamic Antisymmetry. Within this theory, which regards bare small clauses as points of symmetry, *wh*-movement can be traced to the necessity of neutralizing the point of symmetry contained in (42b), which is in fact a small clause. On the other hand, no movement is expected with generalized quantifiers, since they do not constitute a point of symmetry in the structure where they occur. From this point of view, splitting as in *was-für* and *wat-voor* constructions is expected to be the natural option with *wh*-movement as it is for the small clause of a copular sentence. In fact, however, languages differ.

Before we approach the analysis, an important point needs to be spelled out. In copular constructions, as we have seen, the point of symmetry can be neutralized by moving either the subject or the predicate. This is of course possible only if the predicate belongs to the same category as the subject—that is, only if the predicate is a noun phrase. If it is, say, an AP or a PP, the only way to neutralize the point of symmetry is to displace the subject—not because it is a subject but because I^0 selects a noun phrase in its specifier position. In other words, there are no IPs of the type *AP/PP copula DP*.[24] The impossibility of raising AP has nothing to do with Dynamic Antisymmetry; instead, it can be regarded as a restriction based on morphological properties of the head whose specifier the element is moved to. In general, it is not necessary that a point of symmetry yield two solutions, one the mirror image of the other, as in copular constructions of the type *DP copula DP*.

Keeping this caution in mind, let us begin examining *wh*-movement by looking at the derivation of German *was-für* and Dutch *wat-voor* constructions. (I will use the latter for illustration.) In Dutch an overt functional head (*voor*) is available. It is reasonable, then, to assume that the first step in the derivation is to neutralize the point of symmetry constituted by the small clause by moving the *wh*-word (*wat*) to the specifier of *voor*, as in (43); *voor* can be regarded as a counterpart of English *of* in constructions like *this type of books* examined earlier.

(43)

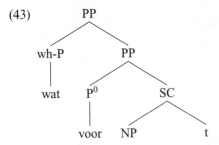

After this move the structure is compatible with the LCA; nevertheless, *wat* moves again, from the specifier of PP to the Comp position of the clause, leaving the residue (*voor* NP) in situ. Why? One possibility is to assume that the landing site is not compatible morphologically with the [+wh] feature of *wat*; thus, *wat* continues moving until it reaches the proper place. However, from a Dynamic Antisymmetry perspective a different explanation should be explored.

In principle, we need to find another element that might constitute a point of symmetry with *wat*, triggering the second movement. There is only one possibility here: the auxiliary *heef* prior to movement to C^0.[25]

(44)

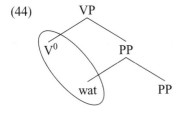

At the stage of the derivation illustrated in (44), the head V^0 c-commands *wat* and *wat* c-commands V^0 (only one segment of PP dominates *wat*); however, this is not sufficient to constitute a point of symmetry. For two nonterminals to constitute a point of symmetry, a further condition must be met: either they both immediately dominate a terminal node or they both dominate a nonterminal node. Since V^0 dominates a terminal node by definition, the structure in (44) can constitute a point of symmetry only if *wat* is a head. We cannot immediately assume that it is, for two reasons: first, the LCA prohibits heads from being specifiers; second, *wat* is holding the place of a full phrase within the small clause. On the other hand, if we simply assume that *wat* is a phrase, the very notion of phrase seems to lose its peculiar content. A phrase is the result of projecting a head. By definition, it should contain complements and/or specifiers; but *wat* never has them. Thus, *wat* is directly reminiscent of clitics in being ambiguous between a head and a phrase. This point deserves a brief digression.

It has long been recognized that clitics have characteristics of both heads and phrases (see Kayne 1984; for a different approach, see Cardinaletti and Starke 1994 and Sportiche 1992). On the one hand, they are heads since they do not contain specifiers or complements and they cannot be used in isolation; on the other, they are phrases since they can occur as complements of heads, they can absorb θ-roles, and they can trigger agreement throughout their chains.[26] Since there is independent evidence that syntax already contains a category ambiguous between heads and maximal projections, let us assume that *wat* can be included in the same class. I will come back to the representation of clitics in syntax in section 3.4.[27]

Assuming this hypothesis to be tenable, we now have a principled reason for the fact that *wat* can constitute a point of symmetry with both a maximal projection in a small clause and a head. Dynamic Antisymmetry then successfully predicts that the *wh*-element moves to a higher position where no other overt element enters into a mutual c-command relation with it. Thus, the split between *wat* and *voor*+NP can be regarded on a par with the inverse copular construction as a case of raising a predicate over the subject mediated by a functional head (cf. *The cause of the riot is these pictures of the wall*).

The problem now is reversed: we must explain what happens when splitting does not occur. To do so, let us look at Italian. Consider a simple sentence like (35c), repeated here as (45).[28]

(45) Quali   libri   hai   letto?
     which.MASC.PL books.MASC.PL have.2SG read
     'Which books have you read?'

Unlike in Dutch, there is no split here, and no preposition. The *wh*-element *quali* and the associated NP *libri* have both raised to the left periphery. However, the same language does show cases of splitting.

(46) a. Quanto   sono alti?
        how.NEUT are   tall.MASC.PL
        'How tall are they?'
   b. *Quanto alti sono?

Is there a reason for this twofold possibility? Let us adopt the small clause analysis we applied to the Dutch case, focusing first on (47).

(47)

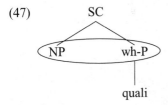

quali

There is a point of symmetry here that must be neutralized, but no particles occur. How can we reconcile the facts with the theory? In principle, an option is immediately open. The *wh*-phrase is adjoined to the small clause itself, as in (48).

(48)

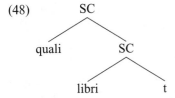

In this position *quali* can c-command the lower NP; but the lower NP cannot c-command *quali* since all segments of the category SC dominate the NP. Thus, *quali* and the NP do not c-command each other and (47) is fully compatible with the LCA. However, this solution raises the same problem concerning selection that we observed with *John reads this type of books*: the idea that a transitive verb like *read* can select a clausal constituent is not (immediately) tenable.

An alternative solution can be proposed involving the occurrence of an abstract D^0. Let us simply reproduce the analysis for *this type of books* and assume that the small clause is selected by an empty functional head, arguably D^0. *Quali* is then raised to the specifier position of DP, as in (49).

(49)

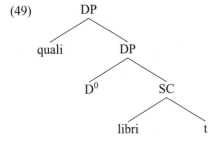

From this position *quali* can c-command out of the DP, and it constitutes a new point of symmetry with the higher V^0 on a par with the Dutch case (recall we are assuming that *wh*-words have a twofold nature, like clitics). The neutralization of this new point of symmetry is different in Italian, though. As we have seen, further movement of the *wh*-phrase triggers pied-piping of the whole constituent in Italian whereas in Dutch the *wh*-phrase can move alone. Why is this so? One explanation for the contrast rests on the licensing conditions on traces. The guiding intuition is that pied-piping is required to license the lower trace; in general, I will essentially follow Rizzi's (1990) theory of locality, requiring traces to be locally governed by a head (either lexically or via agreement; see also Moro 1993).

The structure in (49) is peculiar: the only head governing the lower trace is the (functional head) D^0, since the small clause by definition contains no head at all. This is directly reminiscent of extraction from a bare small clause in copular sentences, which triggers agreement on the verb. This is considered a sufficient strategy to license the lower trace, much as the trace of a preverbal subject is licensed in English via agreement in C^0 (Rizzi 1990). The licensing of the trace in the bare small clause in (49) then must reasonably depend on the capacity of a null D^0 to license the lower trace. If it could not license it, a *that*-trace effect would be expected. Thus, let us assume that an (abstract) agreement relation is established between the *wh*-element and null D^0 on a par with the subject and null C^0 in English. But why can't the *wh*-element then move alone? One possibility is that some further specific restriction is required for a null D^0 to activate agreement. Consider Rizzi's analysis of agreement in the C^0 system. Crosslinguistic analysis shows that agreement in C^0 might involve more than a simple spec-head relation between C^0 and its specifier. A dramatic example is provided by French, where agreement in C^0 is manifest only when C^0 agrees with the head it governs (namely, I^0) and thus C^0 agrees with its IP complement derivatively. In this case the overt complementizer *que* is turned into *qui*. In general, languages can vary according to whether C^0 has intrinsic governing properties or whether more complex structural or morphological conditions are to be met (see Rizzi 1990, sec. 2.5, and references cited there). We can rely on these facts to explain why pied-piping is obligatory. The idea is that a null D^0 is not per se a proper governor and that a further structural condition must be met. Now, since the complement of D^0 is a bare small clause, there is no head with which D^0 can agree, contrary to what happens in the "*que-qui* rule" French case. It is not unreasonable that this further local condition is met in this domain by requiring that the source of agreement for D^0 be locally present: thus, the only possibility is that the *wh*-phrase remains in the specifier of D^0 in order to acquire governing capacities (see Giorgi and Longobardi 1991, chap. 2, for an extensive discussion of government within noun phrases). The plausibility of this analysis can be reinforced by considering contrasts like this one:

(50) a. *Which photographer's did John buy [t D^0 [t pictures of the Pantheon]]?

    b. [Which photographer's D^0 [t pictures of the Pantheon]] did John buy?

Apparently, the D^0 is unable to govern the lower trace without pied-piping. In fact, for most speakers, when the lower D^0 is overt, the structure becomes more acceptable; it becomes totally acceptable when the governing head is the lower lexical head (i.e., *pictures*)—passing through the specifier of DP, as required by Cinque's (1980) generalization (see again Giorgi and Longobardi 1991, chap. 2)—rather than D^0 even if D^0 is empty, supporting the idea that the ungrammaticality of (50) is due to locality conditions on licensing.

(51) Which monument did John buy [(t) D^0 [pictures of t]]?

Although the facts are far from being completely understood, we can reasonably conclude that pied-piping is required by *quali* to preserve the local conditions on the empty category within the bare small clause. More generally, this analysis involving pied-piping could be extended to all cases where an empty D^0 provides a way to neutralize the point of symmetry contained in the bare small clause constituted by a *wh*-phrase and its subject.

    Finally, to support this analysis, recall that Italian has a very low-style alternative to pied-piping, illustrated in (35e) (repeated here as (52)).[29]

(52) Cosa/Quali   hai   letto [t di [libri t]]?
what/which.MASC.PL. have.2SG read   of books
'Which books have you read?'

This alternative in fact parallels the Dutch *wat-voor* construction in that the *wh*-phrase moves out of the small clause via the specifier position of *di*. We could reasonably assume that in this case, as in Dutch, the lower trace is licensed by the overt functional head (here, *di*).

We now have an explanation for why splitting does not take place in Italian with *quali*; yet we must still explain why splitting takes place with *quanto* without the occurrence of any particle like *di*. How can the trace of the *wh*-phrase be licensed in such a case? Consider (35a), repeated here as (53).

(53) Quanto   sono alti?
       how.NEUT are   tall.MASC.PL
       'How tall are they?'

If the analysis of pied-piping based on licensing conditions on traces is correct, we expect the trace of *quanto* to be able to be licensed differently. Rizzi's (1990, see, 2.3.2) analysis of the extraction of measure phrases from AP provides the relevant piece of evidence, which I will reproduce here. Consider the following contrast:

(54) a.   I   palazzi   sono [alti   22 metri].
           the buildings are   high 22 meters
           'The buildings are 22 meters high.'
     b. *I palazzi sono [22 metri alti].

The measure phrase *22 metri* can only appear to the right of the A^0; thus, it is not unreasonable to assume that its trace can be directly governed by the A^0 itself as a lexical head. This analysis is supported on comparative grounds. In English, as the translation of (54a) shows, the measure phrase is basically generated to the left of A^0—to a first approximation, in its specifier position. Thus, extraction involves pied-piping as in the case of Italian *quali*, since no head qualifies as a proper element to license the trace of *how* (see Rizzi 1990).[30]

To summarize this section: We have examined one type of *wh*-movement involving noun phrases and have seen that it can be analyzed, like inverse copular constructions, as a case of predicate raising from a small clause constituent. In both cases movement is required to neutralize a point of symmetry (constituted by the small clause). The difference with respect to quantifiers and articles follows naturally, given the impossibility of analyzing these elements as predicates, both semantically and syntactically, and hence their inability to participate in small clause constructions. Different behaviors are found both across and within languages depending on whether or not overt functional heads (such as *voor*, *für*, and *di*) are involved. If an overt head is available, the natural option is to split the two phrases and raise the *wh*-element alone through the specifier position of the functional head governing the small clause; if there is no overt head, pied-piping is required in order to maintain the proper configuration for licensing the empty category. In all cases examined, the point of symmetry can be neutralized only by moving the *wh*-element. As noted for copular sentences, the absence of an alternative "mirror" strategy (i.e., moving the other pole constituting the point of symmetry while leaving the *wh*-element in situ) can be related to a morphological restriction—the same type of restriction banning movement of the AP in copular constructions to yield structures like *AP copula DP*. More generally, there is no reason to expect a mirror solution to exist for neutralizing all points of symmetry; the possibility of a mirror solution for a point of symmetry in a given language strictly depends on the morphological restrictions holding in that language.

3.3 Multiple-Spec Constructions

Let us return to the abstract schema in (1), illustrating the three potential sources of symmetry in syntax. So far we have reviewed two cases, raising in copular sentences and a class of root *wh*-sentences, where the same type of point of symmetry is involved: (bare) small clauses (1a). A second source of symmetry in syntax is adjunction to a maximal projection as in (1b). Let us first consider this source from a rather abstract point of view.

A basic assumption of X-bar theory is that a head can enter into two types of relations with a maximal projection: head-complement and spec-head. There are various ways to distinguish these two basic relations, according to different analytical perspectives. Agreement, for example, is a typical spec-head relation, whereas categorial selection is generally thought of as a head-complement relation. In general, the unifying concept among different approaches to X-bar theory is c-command asymmetry. Accordingly, a head enters into two distinct types of configuration in terms of c-command: mutual c-command holds between a head and its complement, whereas asymmetric c-command holds between a specifier and a head, for the specifier c-commands the head but is not c-commanded by it. Adjuncts are maximal projections that share with specifiers the fact that they asymmetrically c-command the head; they differ from specifiers in being unable to establish any agreement relation with the head.

As noted earlier, within an LCA framework the distinction between adjuncts and specifiers is no longer tenable. More accurately, since a specifier can c-command out of the maximal projection that contains it, if an adjunct is added to a structure with a specifier, a point of symmetry is generated and the structure is not LCA compatible; this was essentially the case for structure (19) in chapter 2. The consequence is that there can be at most one specifier/adjunct per head or, equivalently, that there is a one-to-one relation between heads and specifiers/adjuncts. By contrast, within Chomsky's (1995) proposal, which maintains the distinction between specifiers and adjuncts, there can be more than one specifier per head, yielding the so-called multiple-spec construction.[31] A Dynamic Antisymmetry approach leads to an intermediate position. On the one hand, within this "weak" version of the antisymmetry theory, Merge can generate multiple-spec constructions, as in Chomsky's proposal; on the other, movement must intervene to leave at most one overt specifier per head, as in Kayne's (1994) proposal, neutralizing all points of symmetry. Notice that this approach maintains the basic intuition that specifiers are in a one-to-one relation with heads. In fact, in order for two or more overt specifiers to occur in a multiple-spec construction, an equal number of heads must be available in the structure, given that all specifiers minus one must be displaced by a movement operation to neutralize the corresponding points of symmetry. Within a Dynamic Antisymmetry approach, then, the one-to-one relation between heads and specifiers is maintained, via movement, although this requirement is now restricted to overt specifiers (regarding nonovert specifiers, see section 3.3.2).

This is the abstract side of the problem. What are the empirical cases of the multiple-spec construction that a Dynamic Antisymmetry analysis can account for? What advantage does this analysis have over other proposals? In section 3.3.1 we will again consider *wh*-movement. Having concentrated previously on the root of *wh*-chains, we will now analyze what happens at the left periphery of a clause structure. In section 3.3.2 we will consider another multiple-spec construction, where we will see the role of empty categories in linearization from a quite different perspective.

3.3.1 On *Do*-Support and Related Matters

The so-called *do*-support phenomenon is a well-known fact of English syntax yielding a sharp partition among arguments. Take a simple case of *wh*-movement in English.

(55) a. Which boy read this book?
     b. Which book did this boy read?

In a matrix clause, when the object is *wh*-moved, an extra head occurs: the inflected verb *do*. This does not happen when the subject is *wh*-moved. *Do*-support phenomena constitute a central topic in the theory of syntax, especially since it has been proved that *do*-support-like phenomena occur productively across languages.[32]

The aim of this section is to illustrate how Dynamic Antisymmetry can account for these facts in a natural way. In fact, it will turn out that Dynamic Asymmetry predicts a more radical subject-object asymmetry. Before we approach the analysis in technical terms, let us consider the issue, as usual, from an abstract point of view. At some level there is a sharp distinction between subjects and objects: subjects are specifiers, objects are complements.[33] Under a Dynamic Antisymmetry approach, when the object is mapped into a specifier position, a point of symmetry is potentially expected since there are now two specifiers: the subject, by definition, and the *wh*-moved object. Thus, under this approach some adjustment in the clause structure is also expected. This is the guideline that will be followed in illustrating *do*-support (and related phenomena) from a Dynamic Antisymmetry perspective. This section is organized in two parts: first, we will concentrate on matrix clauses and see that a Dynamic Antisymmetry analysis offers interesting advantages including selective locality effects; second, we will explore *wh*-movement within and out of subordinate clauses from a rather new perspective.

In fact, the contrast in (55) raises several kinds of questions. In general, there are two possible approaches to the selective occurrence of *do* with the object: either we assume that the subject moves to the same position as the object and then explain why *do* does not occur with the subject, or we assume that the subject, unlike all other arguments, does not move, in which case no special explanation for the absence of *do* with the subject is required. The literature reveals arguments for both approaches.

On the one hand, in the first analysis *wh*-movement to Comp was explained as an interpretive requirement; more specifically, *wh*-movement was regarded as a way to obtain the proper operator-variable relation in natural languages. Such a relation was thought to be implemented in syntax whenever an operator in an Ā-position binds a trace in an A-position. Since adjuncts are by definition Ā-positions, a stronger requirement was necessary to prohibit *wh*-phrases from moving to intermediate adjunct position and stopping there. This stronger requirement was formulated as the *Wh*-Criterion: in order to be interpreted, a *wh*-phrase must be in a spec-head relation with a head containing a [+wh] feature (see

Rizzi 1997 and references cited there). Within the minimalist approach this analysis based on the notion of criterion has been interpreted as a morphological requirement. On this view there is no need to force the grammar to generate an operator-variable configuration; rather, this configuration is the structure resulting from movement of a *wh*-phrase to the specifier of CP to delete uninterpretable features.

On the other hand, empirical evidence was found supporting the alternative hypothesis that the subject does not move. As Chomsky (1986a, 48) writes, "A conclusion consistent with the evidence would be that *wh*-movement takes place except for subjects—that is, the case of 'vacuous movement.' This proposal is developed by George (1980). If we adopt it, then there are a variety of consequences; for example, *wh*-island effects will be removed for embedded *wh*-subjects." In fact, this rather indirect "evidence" is clear from contrasts like this:[34]

(56) a. ?Which book do you wonder [t C^0 [which boy read t]]?
     b. *Which boy do you wonder [which book C^0 [t read t]]?

Since the subject does not move to the specifier of CP, this position is available for the chain of the object (56a); by contrast, since the object does move to the specifier of CP, this position is not available for the chain of the subject. In the latter case the violation of locality conditions on movement is predicted. However, the hypothesis that the subject does not move was problematic, since movement of adjuncts gave the same bad result as extraction of subject across object.

(57) *How do you wonder [which boy read this book t]?

Indeed, if we consider root *wh*-movement of the subject, neither the *Wh*-Criterion nor a morphological theory of movement gives a straightforward account. In fact, the situation is quite paradoxical: on the one hand, one needs to say that the subject uniformly raises to the specifier of CP in order to reach the proper (morphological) environment; on the other, there are good empirical reasons against this conclusion, including the absence of *do*-support. Many efforts have been made to derive the empirical facts and reconcile the two approaches, but I will not review them here. My less ambitious goal is to show how a Dynamic Antisymmetry account sheds light on this issue.

Dynamic Antisymmetry offers an obvious alternative approach to this phenomenon. Earlier we saw that the trigger for *wh*-movement is the necessity of neutralizing a point of symmetry constituted by a *wh*-phrase

—the predicate of a bare small clause selected by D^0—and the lexical
element contained in the small clause. Specifically, the *wh*-phrase moves
to the specifier of DP. Suppose the DP is the object of a transitive verb.
In this case a new point of symmetry is generated involving the verbal
head and the *wh*-element. To neutralize this second point of symmetry,
the *wh*-phrase must move further to a position where no overt head can
c-command it (inducing pied-piping of the whole DP for independent
reasons; see comments on example (49)). In principle, adjunction of the
wh-phrase to IP could be sufficient. Let us look more closely at the configuration that results, shown in (58).

(58)

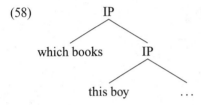

This is a multiple-spec construction—crucially, one that violates the
LCA. The two overt noun phrases c-command each other, precluding
linearization. Thus, *which books* must move to a higher specifier of CP
position, as in (59), to neutralize the point of symmetry.

(59)

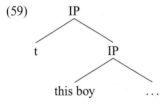

The appearance of *do*-support could then be regarded as a signal that the
wh-phrase has raised to a position that neutralizes the point of symmetry
(perhaps without intermediate adjunction to the IP). In other words, *do*
signals the exploiting of a further layer of clause structure, syncretically
the CP periphery. Notice that Dynamic Antisymmetry only gives us a
natural way to understand why IP is not sufficient; strictly speaking, we
still need to explain why C^0 must be overt. I will come back to this
issue.[35]

Before looking at a possible explanation, let us consider an immediate
empirical advantage of the Dynamic Antisymmetry approach to *do*-
support. What happens in the case of the subject? Let us focus on the
relevant fragment, shown in (60).

(60)

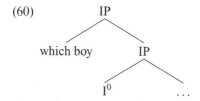

The configuration is now fully compatible with the LCA. There is no need to move *which boy* to a higher specifier of CP because there is no point of symmetry here: the lower I^0 does not c-command *which boy*, since all segments of IP dominate it. In other words, the neutralization of the point of symmetry contained in the bare small clause does not induce further points of symmetry. Movement of *which* to the specifier of DP is sufficient to yield an LCA-compatible structure. Notice that this analysis is not in principle valid across languages. It could well be the case that in certain languages the *wh*-subject moves to higher functional projections—for example, if the C^0 system contains overt material that creates a further point of symmetry to be neutralized. In such a case embedded sentences with *wh*-subjects would be predicted to block *wh*-movement, as embedded sentences with *wh*-objects do. Whether this empirical prediction is correct is a matter that cannot be developed here.

We have seen, then, that a Dynamic Antisymmetry approach accounts naturally for the asymmetry between subjects and objects in *wh*-movement: the subject need not move to the specifier of CP (as opposed to the object), because there is no point of symmetry to be neutralized in this case. This is not the only advantage of such an approach. As noted earlier, two lines of analysis have been pursued: those assuming that all *wh*-phrases move, and those assuming that *wh*-movement does not affect subjects. A Dynamic Antisymmetry approach can be considered an expression of the second trend. Nevertheless, as noted, a theory that excludes movement of *wh*-subjects is paradoxical; it captures the fact that an object can be extracted from an embedded clause with a *wh*-subject, but it does not capture the fact that an adjunct cannot be extracted from an embedded clause with a *wh*-subject on a par with those where the *wh*-phrase is an object (cf. (56)–(57)). The solution that was proposed to amend this theory diminished its force, since it was necessary to assume that the *wh*-subject must move covertly and that locality selectively applies to adjuncts only at LF. The proposal developed here overcomes this difficulty, predicting the locality effect without assuming further covert movement. In fact, this result is based on the LCA definition of movement and the Relativized Minimality approach to locality. Given the definition of c-command adopted for the LCA, a specifier can c-command out of its phrase. In particular, the specifier of a DP can c-command out of the DP (see Kayne 1994, sec. 3.5). This has many welcome consequences. Consider for example the following contrast (taken from Kayne 1994, 24):

(61) a.   [Nobody's [articles]] ever get published fast enough.
     b.   *[Articles by nobody] ever get published fast enough.

Polarity items like *ever* need to be c-commanded by an appropriate licenser (see Larson 1988 and references cited there). The contrast in (61) can be explained easily if we assume that the specifier of the DP can c-command out of its phrase. In (61a) the proper licenser for *ever* is *nobody*; however, in (61b) *nobody* cannot function as a licenser because it does not c-command *ever*. If we combine this fact with a Relativized Minimality approach to locality, we can derive the selective blocking effect of *wh*-phrases on adjuncts. In fact, Rizzi (1990) proves that adjunct chains require both antecedent and head government to be licensed, whereas arguments can skip the antecedent government requirement, because of their intrinsic "referential" force. All in all, since the *wh*-phrase in the specifier of DP of the subject can c-command out of the DP, this is sufficient to block antecedent government of the adjunct. What is relevant here is that this consequence does not require that the *wh*-subject move to the specifier of CP covertly. Thus, the Dynamic Antisymmetry approach to *wh*-movement preserves the advantages of the theory that assumes that only the object moves to the specifier of CP while avoiding the problems that have been discussed.

Before we look at *wh*-movement from and within embedded clauses, one question remains to be addressed. Strictly speaking, Dynamic Antisymmetry explains why the object, but not the subject, needs to move. It does not explain why the head of the specifier hosting the object must be realized overtly. I will not attempt a principled explanation here. I will simply note that this requirement is independent of a theory of movement. We can easily see this by taking into account some independent facts concerning the left periphery of matrix clauses (see also Kayne 1994, sec. 3.6, Rizzi 1997). For now we will simply assume a syncretic model for the CP periphery; later we will need to adopt a more fine-grained analysis, following Rizzi's (1997) proposal. In general, there is no need to realize C^0 overtly. This is typically so in declarative sentences. When the clause has a different force, C^0 might need to be realized overtly (either by insertion of a lexical C^0 or by verb raising). Take for example the contrast between the purely declarative Italian sentence (62a) and its counterparts expressing orders and wishes (62b–e).[36]

(62) a. (*Che) Gianni parte.
           that Gianni leaves
           'Gianni is leaving.'
      b. Op *(che) Gianni parta!
              that Gianni leave
           'I order that Gianni leave.'
      c. Op *(che) Gianni possa partire!
              that Gianni could leave
           'I hope that Gianni leaves.'
      d. *(Se) Gianni potesse partire!
           if   Gianni could leave
           'If only Gianni could leave.'
      e. Potesse/Possa Gianni t partire.
         could   Gianni   leave
           'I hope that Gianni leaves.'

As a first approximation, we can assume that in the nondeclarative sentences the specifier of the topmost head of the clause structure is occupied by a null operator (Op) ranging over the set of values that C^0 can take. If this is correct, *do*-support is just a special case of this general pattern; the major relevant difference is that the operator (the object *wh*-phrase) is overt. Arguably, then, the overt realization of C^0 should not be accounted for by a theory of movement.

To summarize the analysis so far: A well-known asymmetry between subjects and objects in root *wh*-sentences can be naturally explained in a Dynamic Antisymmetry framework. When the object is fronted (to neutralize the point of symmetry contained in the bare small clause constituted by the *wh*-element and the noun phrase), a further point of symmetry with the subject is generated; thus, it must be moved to a higher position that asymmetrically c-commands it. There is no need to move the subject to the same high position because no further point of symmetry is created to neutralize the point of symmetry contained in it. Overt realization of C^0 (by insertion of *do*) is then independently required for objects only, as in all matrix clauses involving an operator in the specifier of CP.

In the rest of this section we will explore *wh*-movement from and within embedded sentences. Dealing with this issue will require revising the analysis offered for root sentences, although the spirit of that analysis will be fully maintained.

Let us focus on two simple cases of *wh*-movement involving embedded sentences.

(63) a. John wonders [[which books] [Mary read]].
     b. [[Which books] [does John believe that Mary read]]?

At a rather primitive level of analysis, these sentences represent two opposite alternatives: the *wh*-phrase must stay in the subordinate clause (63a) or it must move to the left periphery of the root clause (63b). From a Dynamic Antisymmetry perspective, it must be the case that in (63b) a point of symmetry has pushed the *wh*-phrase to that position. We also know that the *wh*-phrase in (63a) has moved to the specifier position of an abstract head; if it were simply adjoined to IP, a point of symmetry would be created with the subject. Two separate questions can be distinguished here: What triggers movement of the *wh*-phrase from the embedded clause in (63b)? and How is the point of symmetry neutralized in the embedded clause in (63a)? Let us approach these questions separately.

An obvious account of the neutralization of the point of symmetry in (63a) would assume that the object has moved to the specifier of CP; if it had not, it would constitute a point of symmetry with the subject. Paralleling the case of root sentences, a *wh*-subject would not need to move, because no further points of symmetry are created when the *wh*-predicate (*which*) raises to the specifier of DP, neutralizing the point of symmetry contained in it. A new question arises: if *which books* were in the specifier of CP, we would expect a further point of symmetry between *wonders* and *which*, hence further movement of the *wh*-phrase. One way to justify the absence of further movement would be to adopt a richer CP layer representation.

Like the structure of the other two major clausal "fields," IP and VP, the structure of CP has recently been rethought. The lexical (VP) and inflectional (IP) layers were originally analyzed as single X-bar projections. The necessity of accounting for more complex data led to a much more fine-grained analysis whereby each syncretic head (I^0 and V^0) was scattered in a series of single (overt or covert) feature specifications, each with the same X-bar skeleton. Following Pollock's (1989) seminal work (see also Moro 1988), the IP layer was essentially decomposed into the features of the verbal conjugation (Agr, Asp, T, etc.). The VP layer was decomposed into more abstract units, including the so-called light verb phrase (*v*P), in an effort to construct a binary-branching representation of multiple-argument verbs (see Larson 1988, Hale and Keyser 1993). CP has also been decomposed into smaller units.

The complementizer system minimally consists of a specification of force, accessible to higher selection, and a specification of finiteness selecting a finite (or nonfinite) IP. It may also consist of a topic and a focus field, expressing the topic-comment and focus-presupposition articulations respectively. (Rizzi 1997, 325)

Structurally, the CP layer can be represented as follows:

(64) CP = ... $Force^0$ ... (Top^0) ... (Foc^0) ... (Top^0) ... Fin^0 IP

Rizzi continues:

Different types of elements fill different positions in [(64)]. Straightforward distributional evidence suggests that relative pronouns are in the spec of $Force^0$, while interrogative pronouns in main questions compete with focussed phrases for the spec of $Focus^0$. Complementizers such as *that*, *que*, etc. are in $Force^0$ (when the topic-focus field is activated), while prepositional complementizers in Romance are in Fin^0. (Rizzi 1997, 325)

Thus, one way to explain why the *wh*-phrase in the object in (63a) does not constitute a further point of symmetry with the matrix verb *wonder* would be to say that *wonder* selects an interrogative feature [+wh] in the complementizer it selects.[37] Under a multiple-head analysis of the CP layer, this would be implemented by including an abstract head that would protect the *wh*-phrase from constituting a point of symmetry with the matrix verb, hence from further movement. We will see that this simple explanation, represented in (65), cannot be maintained.

(65) ... wonder ... F^0 [which books F^0 ...

Let us now turn to (63b). The object cannot be an adjunct to the embedded IP because it would constitute a point of symmetry with the subject, so it needs to move higher. Since we are assuming that *believe*, unlike *wonder*, does not select an abstract empty head, the object can only move to the left periphery of the root clause. This could work for objects, but what about subjects? Subjects should never move, since there is no other specifier with which they constitute a point of symmetry. We could say that the overt complementizer *that* creates a point of symmetry with the *wh*-phrase in the specifier of DP, but once we adopt the multiple-head analysis for the CP layer (to account for *wonder*), we would predict that if *that* instantiating Force^0 were separated from the *wh*-subject by, say, a topic element, the subject would not need to move. In fact, the specifier of the subject (*which*) would c-command and be c-commanded by Fin^0; since Fin^0 is not overt, there would be no point of symmetry to be neutralized, hence no movement. However, this is not the case.

(66) *John believes (that) ... yesterday Top^0 ... Fin^0 which girls read this book

The conclusion is straightforward: movement of an embedded *wh*-phrase cannot be directly related to the structure of the left periphery since the latter might contain (many) empty heads that would prevent movement. If we want to maintain Dynamic Antisymmetry, there is only one option left, namely, that the point of symmetry that triggers *wh*-movement from embedded sentences is related to the IP system itself. Before approaching the analysis from a technical point of view, we need to reconsider the way predication is implemented in syntax.

So far we have implicitly assumed that bare small clauses are not the only predicative structures. More specifically, we have assumed that IPs are interpreted as predicative structures along with small clauses. Let us make the theory more restrictive by assuming that all and only bare small clauses instantiate a predicative linking. Accordingly, let the link between a noun phrase and IP be a bare small clause, not an asymmetric projection of IP.[38]

(67)

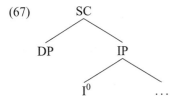

What is the consequence of this radical assumption? Since we are now assuming that all sentences contain a point of symmetry to be neutralized, we need to rethink root clauses accordingly. An obvious question arises concerning agreement with the verb (as mediated by the I^0 system). In fact, there is no compelling reason why the subject could not agree with the head of IP even if the subject is not an adjunct to IP. Indeed, we must independently assume that agreement can be established between the subject and the predicate in bare small clauses of copular sentences without the intervention of (a spec-head relation with) a functional head (see section 3.2.1). Assuming that this hypothesis is tenable, let us explore its empirical consequences; more specifically, let us explore what strategies are exploited to neutralize the point of symmetry constituted by the subject and the predicate in different types of clause. In the rest of this section we will look first at root clauses and then at embedded clauses. We will see that a Dynamic Antisymmetry approach requires adopting radically different structural representations for those cases where the *wh*-phrase can remain within the subordinate clause and those where it moves up to the root left periphery.

Let us address a preliminary question. How can the point of symmetry in (67) be neutralized? The version of c-command embodied in the LCA suggests a simple answer: it can be neutralized by adjoining the subject to the bare small clause, as in (68). From this position it asymmetrically c-commands the bare small clause and its content (notice that IP cannot c-command any element adjoined to the bare small clause).

(68)

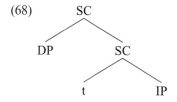

In principle, this would be enough. Notice that this is still consistent with the multiple-head analysis of the CP system. Within a fine-grained approach to the structure of the left periphery, adjunction is assumed not to be free in the CP layer; if it were, all major generalizations would be lost. Accordingly, we cannot assume adjunction in the space between $Force^0$ and Fin^0. However, we have not committed ourselves on whether adjunction can take place lower than Fin^0 (and higher than $Force^0$), pace, of course, the LCA. Let us assume, then, that adjunction (by arguments) is possible in the space below Fin^0, as instantiated in (68).

To summarize the analysis so far: The goal is to find a plausible way to interpret *wh*-movement within and from embedded sentences as a consequence of neutralizing a point of symmetry. We first established that no point of symmetry can be created between the *wh*-arguments and the left periphery of the embedded sentence itself, since the latter may contain abstract empty heads. We then pursued the opposite possibility, that a point of symmetry can be created below the left periphery at the level of the IP system.

To prove that this hypothesis is empirically relevant, we will now proceed as usual: assuming that Dynamic Antisymmetry is correct, we will try to interpret movement as a way of neutralizing the point of symmetry. We will see that Dynamic Antisymmetry forces us to assume a radically different view of clausal complementation for embedded interrogatives. A list of the core cases, focusing on subjects for the sake of simplicity, is provided in (69).

(69) a. This boy read a book.
   b. Which boy read a book?
   c. John believes (that) this boy read a book.
   d. Which boy does John believe C^0 read a book?
   e. John wonders which boy read a book.

From a Dynamic Antisymmetry perspective, it must be the case that in each sentence the points of symmetry constituted by the subject and IP can be neutralized, yielding the observed linear order. Let us assume that this is so and consider the situation in detail. In (69a) adjunction of a [−wh] argument (*this boy*) to the bare small clause complement of a root empty [−wh] C^0 neutralizes the point of symmetry; in (69b) adjunction of a [+wh] argument (*which boy*) to the small clause complement of a root empty [+wh] C^0 is also successful; and in the embedded declarative (69c) adjunction of a [−wh] argument (*this boy*) to the small clause complement of an embedded [−wh] C^0, either overt or empty, must be possible as well. On the other hand, the same strategy must not be viable in (69d): it must be the case that *which boy* cannot be adjoined to the small clause complement of the embedded C^0 and thus it is moved to the higher specifier of CP (cf. **John believes which boy read a book?*). What distinguishes this case from (69b) and (69c)? In this case a [+wh] argument adjoins to a [−wh] C^0 selected by a higher verb. Why should this be blocked? I would like to suggest that this restriction is to be traced to the specific properties that govern selection (or Agree, in Chomsky's (2000) terms). In (69d) the embedded complementizer C^0 is selected by the matrix verb V^0 under government and assigned a [−wh] feature. If *which boy* were adjoined to the bare small clause, the small clause would no longer dominate it (only one segment would), and *which* would c-command out of the small clause. Thus, the matrix verb *believe* would govern two heads, namely, a [−wh] C^0 and a [+wh] *which* (recall that we are assuming *which* has a twofold nature); it is not unreasonable that the incompatibility of *believe* with two opposite values for the same feature (in the same local domain) is what makes this strategy to neutralize the point of symmetry unavailable, forcing movement to the left periphery of the root clause. Let us now turn to (69e); here, adjunction to the small clause complement of the embedded C^0 is viable. Why should this be so? Technically speaking, there could be a consistent solution based on selection. One might assume that unlike *believe*, *wonder* is able to select a [+wh] C^0; hence, no conflict would arise. Nevertheless, from an explanatory point of view, this solution does not appear satisfactory. In fact, it would just amount to shifting the problem entirely to the level of the lexicon. Of course, this move would not be incorrect per se; there must be distinct lexical properties that distinguish *believe* and *wonder*. Rather, the problem is that there is no obvious way to test the assumption concerning the selection of a [±wh] complementizer on independent grounds. I would like to suggest a different solution that will allow such an independent test.

Let us first assume that there can be no lexical variation with respect to the assignment of a [±wh] feature to a C^0 by a verb: if a C^0 is governed by a verb, it can only be [−wh] (regarding government, see note 8 of the appendix). To put it somewhat informally, let us assume that questions cannot be complements. This is the crucial assumption on which I will ground the argument. The assumption gains support from the following contrast:

(70) a. *John believes [which books Mary read].
     b.   John believes [[which books Mary read] to be evident].

It is not intrinsically incompatible for a question (i.e., a [+wh] clause) to be in the domain of *believe*; what is to be excluded is that *believe* govern a [+wh] C^0, which is not the case in (70). Bearing this in mind, let us return to the problem of distinguishing *believe* and *wonder*. What would the impact of this assumption, that questions cannot be complements, be for what matters here? Since there can hardly be a doubt that the C^0 following *wonder* is endowed with a [+wh] feature, only one possibility remains: namely, that *believe* and *wonder* must be assigned the distinct structures shown in (71a) and (71b).

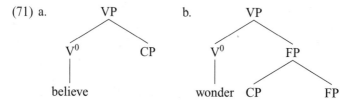

(71) a.

We will come back to FP; for now let us concentrate on the immediate advantages of this alternative representation and ensure that it allows us to capture the difference between (69d) and (69e). In fact, it does. In (71a) the matrix verb governs C^0 (and CP); hence, C^0 must be [−wh]. By contrast, in (71b) the matrix verb does not govern C^0. Instead, it governs F^0 and FP; hence, C^0 can be [+wh]. Thus, the method of neutralizing the point of symmetry is expected to differ for the two embedded clauses. It cannot be neutralized by adjunction to the embedded C^0 in (71a) because a feature conflict would result. It *can* be neutralized by adjunction to the embedded C^0 in (71b) because C^0 is not governed by the matrix verb and hence can host a [+wh] feature. Mutatis mutandis, the strategy for neutralizing the point of symmetry in (71b) would parallel the one used for root clauses like (69b): namely, it can exploit the immediately available left periphery. In fact, as with root clauses, this conclusion is also consistent with the hypothesis that the subject can stay in a lower position with *wonder* whereas the object raises to the specifier of CP, yielding the selective locality effects illustrated in (56)–(57).[39]

Let us now evaluate the proposal. As noted, the question is whether there are independent reasons to assume the different structure for *wonder* shown in (71b). I would like to suggest that there are indeed such reasons by rethinking locality effects on extraction from *wonder*. The guiding intuition here is that extraction from the CP following *wonder* is expected to yield violations, as is extraction from a subject position. Let us consider some core cases.

As noted earlier, it is well known that extraction from the CP complement of *wonder*, unlike extraction from the CP complement of *believe*, yields a typical Subjacency violation. In general, extraction from the CP complement of *believe* is illicit if the intermediate specifier of CP position hosts overt material. For example, compare extraction of an object with extraction of an adjunct.

(72) a. ?*Which books do you wonder how C^0 John read t?
   b. *How do you wonder which books C^0 John read t t?

The differing acceptability of (72a) and (72b) is standardly accounted for by assuming that adjunct chains require both antecedent and head government to be licensed whereas arguments do not require antecedent government, because of their intrinsic "referential" force (Rizzi 1990). Now, the relevant fact is that extraction from the complement of *wonder* still gives a weakly ungrammatical result (typically associated with Subjacency violations) even if no overt *wh*-element occupies the intermediate specifier of CP position and whether or not an overt complementize occurs.

(73) ?*Which books do you wonder (if/whether) John read t?

One way to trace the ungrammaticality of (73) to Subjacency is obviously to assume that the specifier position of the embedded CP is occupied by an abstract null operator (Op) with *wonder*, preventing movement of the *wh*-chain through the intermediate position. This would contrast with the case of *believe*, where no Op is introduced in the specifier of CP and that position is therefore available for the *wh*-chain.

(74) a. *?Which books do you wonder Op (if/whether) John read t?
     b.   Which books do you believe t that John read t?

I will not address the important issue of the status of null Op in syntax and the reasons why it is obligatory with *wonder* and impossible with *believe*.[40] What is relevant here is that, if we adopt the structures in (71), the contrast between *wonder* and *believe* follows without assuming any special Op. Consider first the following contrast (cf. also (70b)):

(75) a.   Which books does John believe [t that Mary read t]?
     b. *?Which books does John believe [[t that Mary read t] to be evident]?

In (75b) the extraction from the embedded CP yields a typical Subjacency violation, whereas in (75a) no locality condition is violated. This immediately suggests a way to interpret the Subjacency violation that occurs when extracting from the complement of *wonder*: extraction yields a Subjacency violation because it takes place from the same structural position as the extraction in (75b), namely, from subject position. We thus have independent evidence to support the distinction that Dynamic Antisymmetry has forced us to assume in (71).

As for the nature of the FP constituent that is the complement of *wonder*, I would tentatively like to suggest that this is the same kind of abstract predicate found in constructions like (76).

(76)

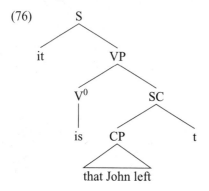

This sentence (an inverse copular sentence; see the appendix) has an emphatic sense if compared with its noncopular counterpart (*John left*). In Moro 1997b, chap. 3, I suggest that the absence of an overt predicate (syntactically realized by the occurrence of a propredicative *it*, for EPP-like reasons) is interpreted as a propositional predicate of the kind *The fact is that p*, *It's true that p*, and so on. I would like to suggest that the empty FP occurring with *wonder* in (71b) is interpreted in the same way as a propositional predicate in (76). Intuitively, a question like *John wonders if p* is interpreted as 'John wonders if p is true'. The absence of any expletive is to be related to the fact that *wonder*, unlike *be*, assigns a thematic role to the subject; hence, the subject position is independently filled.

Finally, notice that the approach based on the two abstract structures in (71) would allow us to explore the lexicon in a quite interesting way. Along with verbs like *believe* and *wonder*, which can only be associated with structure (71a) and structure (71b), respectively, there are verbs like *say*, *know*, and *predict* for which both options are available.

(77) a.   John wonders who read the book.
     b.   *?Who does John wonder (if) read the book?
     c.   *John believes who read the book.
     d.   Who does John believe read the book?
     e.   John says who read the book.
     f.   Who does John say read the book?

The next step would be to consider whether sentences like (77e) with *say* have the same type of structure as those with *wonder*, hence whether the locality effect of extraction from the embedded clause is amenable to the same kind of structural explanation. However, such research is beyond the limits of this book. For present purposes it is sufficient to recognize that the different structures a Dynamic Antisymmetry perspective forces us to adopt for *believe* and *wonder* are supported by independent evidence.

To summarize: We started by interpreting the subject/object asymmetry with *do*-support as the consequence of the differing status of subjects, which are specifiers, and objects, which are complements. *Do*-support shows up with objects because when an object is moved, it becomes a specifier and creates a further point of symmetry with another specifier, namely, the subject. The occurrence of *do* is the result of the object's need to reach a higher specifier position. The subject does not move higher, and *do* is not inserted, because the structure contains no other specifier with which the subject can create a point of symmetry.

We then looked at *wh*-movement within and from embedded sentences, considering two questions: What triggers movement in embedded clauses? and How is the point of symmetry neutralized? We discarded a first simple hypothesis that movement is triggered by the left periphery of the embedded clause and explored the conjecture that it is the result of a point of symmetry created at the IP level. To implement this conjecture, we adopted a restrictive theory of predication and assumed that only bare small clauses (which are points of symmetry) instantiate a predicative linking in all clauses. We then noted that *wh*-movement follows as a way to neutralize a point of symmetry provided that the structure of clausal complementation is refined: specifically, provided that (unlike the CP following *believe*) the CP following *wonder* is not its complement but the specifier of a more complex structure. Finally, we saw that this distinction between *wonder* and *believe*, originally forced by Dynamic Antisymmetry, has independent empirical advantages in that locality violation effects (specifically, selective blocking effects for adjuncts and objects and Subjacency violations) naturally follow from the phrase structure representations.

3.3.2 Rightward Agreement in Italian and the Role of Empty Categories

This section has a major theoretical aim: to reinforce a central theoretical hypothesis of Dynamic Antisymmetry, namely, that empty categories do not interfere with linearization. More specifically, we have so far assumed that multiple-spec constructions constitute a typical trigger for movement. Replacing an overt specifier/adjunct with a trace neutralizes the point of symmetry, overcoming the problems related to linearization of overt categories. In principle, one could object that movement is inherently related to the nature of traces (i.e., one could object that it is some specific, as-yet-undiscovered property of traces that makes them neutralize a point of symmetry); or one could think that the structures analyzed here trigger movement per se, whether or not linearization is required (e.g., one could assume that multiple-spec constructions trigger movement per se). What type of empirical case would support our line of reasoning? The answer is that a multiple-spec construction involving a base-generated empty category that does not trigger movement would support the assumption that the only role of traces in movement is that of neutralizing a point of symmetry. To find such a construction, we will explore the rather murky issue of verbal agreement in pro-drop languages—in particular, verbal agreement in (inverse) copular sentences.

A fundamental assumption of syntactic theory is that verb agreement with the subject is established as a relation with the I^0 system. Formally, this is commonly represented by a spec-head relation between the DP subject and I^0.

(78)

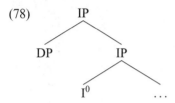

In the previous section we explored the hypothesis that the predicative link between the subject and the IP system is implemented as a bare small clause as in (67), rather than a two-segment projection of IP as in (78). Since this hypothesis plays an effective role only in the case of subordination, we can adopt the more familiar representation for the sake of simplicity.

Now consider a nominal small clause as selected by the copula. Following the unified theory of copular sentences illustrated in the appendix, we can assume that (for a proper choice of DPs) either the subject or the predicative DP can be raised to the specifier of IP, yielding a canonical or an inverse copular sentence, respectively. Consider two DPs like these, differing in number:

(79) a. $[_{DP}$ these pictures$]_{+pl}$
   b. $[_{DP}$ the cause of the riot$]_{+sg}$

The question is, what kind of verb agreement will DP-raising yield in canonical and inverse copular sentences? The result is a clear contrast.

(80) a. [These pictures$]_{+pl}$ are$_{+pl}$ [t the cause of the riot].
   b. [The cause of the riot$]_{+sg}$ is$_{+sg}$ [these pictures t].

Clearly, each DP constituting the predicative linking in the small clause preserves its own number and determines verb agreement.[41] This is hardly surprising, if we follow the fundamental assumption on verbal agreement mentioned at the start of this section. Filling in the slots of the I^0 system with the DPs in question, as shown in (81), let us focus on the relevant segments.

(81) a.

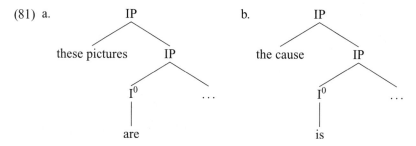

Since verb agreement is established by a spec-head relation with (some head contained in) the I^0 system, matching of the verb with the preverbal DP is obvious. Nominal small clauses do confirm the general pattern. However, reproducing the same type of experiment in Italian yields surprising results. Consider the following Italian paradigm and the English translations in quotation marks.

(82) a. [$_{IP}$[$_{DP}$ Queste foto   del   muro] sono [$_{SC}$ t la   causa della
            these   pictures of-the wall   are   the cause of-the
        rivolta]].
        riot
        'These pictures of the wall are the cause of the riot.'
    b. [$_{IP}$[$_{DP}$ La causa della   rivolta] sono [$_{SC}$ queste foto   del
            the cause of-the riot   are   these   pictures of-the
        muro t]].
        wall
        'The cause of the riot is these pictures of the wall.'

This paradigm shows that in Italian the copula is always plural when the subject of the predication (*queste foto del muro*) is plural, even in cases where this phrase follows the copula. This raises a nontrivial problem. If we do not want to abandon the fundamental assumption that verb agreement with the subject is ultimately established as a spec-head relation with the I^0 system, we must conclude that in (82b) the preverbal predicative DP is not in the specifier of IP. In other words, we cannot adopt for Italian the equivalent (83) of (81b), because *la causa* is singular whereas *sono* is plural.

(83)

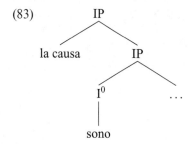

If *la causa* were in the specifier of IP, it should trigger agreement on I^0, yielding third singular *è* 'is' rather than third plural *sono* 'are'. Two questions arise: First, what occupies the specifier of IP? Second, where is the preverbal DP *la causa*? A detailed answer to these questions would take us too far afield. For present purposes it is sufficient to point out two main results of the arguments developed in Moro 1997b, sec. 1.3.3.3.2.

A natural candidate to be the occupant of the specifier of IP is *pro*. The analysis of copular sentences in Moro 1997b (including the equivalent of *there*-sentences in Italian, namely, *ci*-sentences) shows that *pro* is always present in Italian (even in noncopular sentences). If this is correct, the underlying structure of (82b) is as follows, including *pro* in the specifier of IP:

(84) pro sono [$_{SC}$[$_{DP}$ queste foto del muro] [$_{DP}$ la causa della rivolta]]

Notice that the resulting agreement between the two DPs *pro* and *queste foto del muro* can be regarded as the same kind of agreement found in copular constructions involving overt pronouns, such as *Gianni e Maria sono loro* 'Gianni and Maria are them'. The fact that *pro* "agrees" with *queste foto del muro* rather than with *la causa della rivolta* is a reasonable result of the asymmetric nature of the two DPs in terms of predicational properties: *queste foto* is the fully referential DP, whereas *la causa* is the predicate. Thus, it is not unreasonable to assume that *pro* has the same features as the subject rather than the predicate. If (84) is the underlying structure of copular sentences, then there is no exception to the standard claim that verb agreement with the subject is ultimately established as a spec-head relation with the I^0 system. As independently suggested in Moro 1997b, the only specific assumption is that *pro* must be obligatory.

Now let us take up the second question: what position *la causa della rivolta* occupies in (82b). Clearly, movement has occurred. The bare small clause contains a point of symmetry that must be neutralized. In fact, (84) is not grammatical at all as is; one of the DPs must move. Let us concentrate on the inverse sentence. As a first approximation, the structure in (82b) could be enriched by adding *pro*, as follows:

(85) ... [$_{DP}$ la causa della rivolta] ... pro sono [$_{SC}$[$_{DP}$ queste foto del muro] t]

The point of symmetry is now neutralized; however, we still do not know where the raised predicate has landed. The question can be further sharpened. We know that the predicate cannot have landed in the specifier of IP; if it had, it would have triggered verb agreement. There are two possible solutions: either it moved to some slot available in the Comp periphery or it adjoined to IP. Assuming the scattered CP theory and the diagnostic proposed in Rizzi 1997, there are a number of facts we must check to exclude the possibility that *la causa della rivolta* has reached the left periphery—specifically, the specifier position of any functional heads within the CP layer. Here again is the basic structure:

(86) $CP = \dots Force^0 \dots (Top^0) \dots (Foc^0) \dots (Top^0) \dots Fin^0$ IP

Now consider the following cases:

(87) a. Gianni dice che la causa della rivolta sono queste foto
         Gianni says that the cause of-the riot   are these pictures
         del   muro.
         of-the wall
         'Gianni says that the cause of the riot is these pictures of the wall.'
    b. * Gianni dice la causa della rivolta che sono queste foto
         Gianni says the cause of-the riot   that are   these pictures
         del   muro.
         of-the wall
    c. La causa della rivolta, queste foto   lo sono certo.
        the cause of-the riot   these pictures LO are   certainly
    d. * LA CAUSA DELLA RIVOLTA sono QUESTE FOTO.
         the cause   of-the riot   are these   pictures
    e. essendo la causa della rivolta t queste foto
        being   the cause of-the riot   these pictures
    f. * la causa della rivolta essendo queste foto   del   muro
         the cause of-the riot   being   these pictures of-the wall

First, the relative order of *la causa della rivolta* and *che* (which is taken to be the overt realization of $Force^0$) in (87a–b) indicates that *la causa della rivolta* cannot have reached $Force^0$. In fact, if the sentence is embedded, declarative C^0 (*che*) precedes rather than follows it. Second, it can be shown that *la causa della rivolta* is not in the specifier of TopP. In Romance languages topic-comment structures are typically expressed by clitic left dislocation (CLLD) constructions (see Cinque 1990 and references cited there). Indeed, one can construct a topic-comment structure with *la causa della rivolta* as topic (see (87c)), but the sentence would include a clitic, which is plainly not the case in (85). Third, *la causa della rivolta* cannot be in the specifier of FocP. Inverse copular sentences are characterized by a special property: the lower subject is focused. Although a precise analysis of subverbal focus is still to be developed (see Belletti 1999 and Longobardi 1999 for an advanced proposal on VP-related focus positions), this fact surely excludes the possibility that a raised predicate in an inverse copular construction is focused, since Focus cannot occur twice in the same monoclausal sentence (e.g., *IL LIBRO, A MARIA, Gianni dà 'The book, to Maria, Gianni gives'; see Rizzi 1997 for a discussion on the uniqueness of Focus based on quantificational considerations). Thus, (87d) shows that la causa della rivolta cannot be in Foc^0. Finally, if we test Aux-to-Comp constructions, we observe that the auxiliary precedes the predicative noun phrase as in (87e). Since Aux-to-Comp constructions involve movement of the auxiliary to FinP, we can exclude the possibility that la causa della rivolta is in the specifier of FinP. We are left with the only residual possibility: that la causa della rivolta has been adjoined to IP. Thus, (85) can be completed as follows:

(88) C^0 [$_{IP}$[$_{DP}$ la causa della rivolta] [$_{IP}$ pro sono [$_{SC}$[$_{DP}$ queste foto del muro] t]]]

This offers us the central empirical datum of this section. Consider the following fragment of the structure:

(89)

This is a clear example of a multiple-spec construction—crucially, one where two phrases, la causa della rivolta and pro, c-command each other. This configuration violates the LCA; compare it with the one in (90) related to wh-movement.

(90)

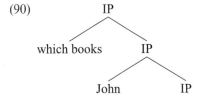

Here, only movement of which books can rescue the structure. In (89), as noted, la causa della rivolta does not move further. This is not a contradiction of a Dynamic Antisymmetry–based approach. In fact, *pro* is an empty category; thus, Dynamic Antisymmetry correctly predicts that no movement is triggered since there is no need to neutralize the point of symmetry. Notice that if *pro* were replaced as in (91) by its overt counterpart, the feminine plural pronoun *esse*, the sentence would not be acceptable.

(91)

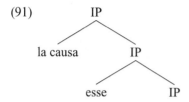

Thus, we can claim that inverse copular sentences in Italian are clearly multiple-spec constructions. The lexical items are arranged in such a way that the predicate adjoins to IP, in whose specifier *pro* is activated for independent reasons. The reason why movement is not triggered is that it is forced only if a point of symmetry is created by overt elements. Since *pro* is null, movement is unnecessary. This phenomenon indirectly reinforces my proposed approach to movement on theoretical grounds. The role of traces is to rescue LCA-incompatible structures. The absence of movement in a point of symmetry containing a base-generated empty category confirms this approach.[42]

To summarize: In this section we explored a second possible source of symmetry between two maximal projections: multiple-spec constructions (1b). We analyzed independent instances of multiple-spec constructions in a unified way (focusing on *wh*-movement in English and predicate raising in Italian), concluding that movement is triggered to neutralize a point of symmetry only if the specifiers involved are both phonologically realized. This offers indirect theoretical support to Dynamic Antisymmetry, since it shows that movement is inherently related to linearization, relying on the assumption that empty categories do not need to be linearized. In the next section we will look at the third possible source of symmetry identified in (1): the one constituted by two heads.

3.4 Head-Head Constructions

Let us start, as usual, from the abstract point of view. A potential source of symmetry is a configuration like (1c), repeated here as (92).

(92)   XP

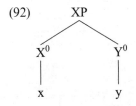

The two nonterminals X^0 and Y^0 c-command each other and immediately dominate the two terminals x and y; thus, there is no way to linearize x and y.[43] Plainly, (92) is not compatible with the LCA because X^0 and Y^0 constitute a point of symmetry. However, if we assume a weak antisymmetry approach such as Dynamic Antisymmetry, this structure can be generated as (1a–b) can, provided that movement rescues it by neutralizing the point of symmetry before the structure is spelled out. Notice that the reason why movement intervenes to rescue this structure is quite different from the reason why it intervenes to rescue structures (1a–b). In fact, from a Dynamic Antisymmetry perspective, there is a substantial conceptual distinction between this source of symmetry and the previous ones involving maximal projections. As suggested in section 3.1, in structure (92) there is no conflict over how to linearize the terminals. Rather, there is no pair of nonterminals such that one asymmetrically c-commands the other. This is equivalent to saying that there is no way to linearize x and y, not that the linear order is paradoxical. This has a notable theoretical consequence: in such a case movement (i.e., chain formation) appears to be primitive with respect to linear order in that movement induces linear order, which would otherwise not be determinable.[44]

In this section I will suggest that the abstract structure in (92) generated by weak antisymmetry is in fact empirically relevant as the trigger for clitic movement. The argument is divided in two parts. First, I will approach the more general problem of representing clitics (within an LCA framework). Second, I will approach a specific empirical issue, namely, the distinction between clitics and stressed pronouns in Italian, showing what lines of reasoning a Dynamic Antisymmetry framework suggests.

3.4.1   Clitics, Nonbranching Projections, and Movement
Within the standard X-bar theory, (92) is simply banned by requiring that a phrase cannot immediately contain two heads. Indeed, the fact that two heads cannot be directly merged could also be derived in the standard framework using a number of assumptions that are conceptually independent from X-bar-theoretical considerations, such as selectional properties and θ-role structures. Let us focus on θ-role structure, beginning

with a simple example involving a sequence of two heads like *John knows stories*. The fragment ... *knows stories* ... is potentially a candidate for a structure like (92); in fact, *knows* and *stories* could have been merged without any intermediate structure. θ-theory can exclude that possibility. The information contained in lexical items (heads) includes thematic relations as implemented within X-bar structures (see Hale and Keyser 1993 and references cited there). Thus, the lexical information associated with a noun like *stories* specifies that this item is compatible with two distinct thematic relations (agent and patient, as in *John's stories about Mary*). Assuming (some version of) Hale and Keyser's (1993) theory, each thematic relation is implemented by the geometry of the X-bar structure: a patient is c-commanded by the head, the agent is not, and so on. Thus, one way to bar ... *knows stories* ... from instantiating (92) is to say that a head like *stories* cannot simply suspend the pieces of thematic information it is assigned in the lexicon, hence the pieces of X-bar structure associated with it: when it occurs alone, the structure is present, although the slots are not filled by any argument.

Within a minimalist approach to phrase structure (bare phrase structure, in Chomsky's (1995) terms), conceptually different arguments are needed to exclude structures like (92). Recall that within such a framework no information is visible to Merge except lexical features (including of course phonological information). Simply saying that *stories* can be considered as a maximal projection by Merge, then, would not be consistent; on the other hand, the relevant information cannot be expressed as a "feature," unless, of course, one wants to consider a piece of X-bar structure information as a "feature." For bare nouns to be possible, then, the theory is forced to assume that their occurrence is always accompanied by some hidden functional structure that prevents (92) from being generated—for example, an extra D^0. Similar considerations hold for nouns that do not project any thematic structure, such as, prototypically, proper names and pronouns. Whether or not this assumption is viable (see Chierchia 1993, Longobardi 1994, Carlson and Pelletier 1995, and references cited there for extensive discussion on the nature of bare plurals and proper names), the simplicity gained by assuming a bare phrase structure framework is diminished by the necessity of assuming more complex abstract entities.

Within an LCA approach, taking phrase markers as autonomous entities, nothing prevents us from saying that the complex X-bar structure associated with *stories* is preserved even when it occurs with no arguments. In other words, we can simply say that *stories* is dominated by more than one nonterminal node even when it occurs with no arguments; hence, (92) is easily avoided. Indeed, this claim must also apply to nouns like proper names that do not project thematic structure. In fact, Kayne (1994, 9) simply adopts the view that a proper name is dominated by (at least) another node, thus excluding a structure like (92), as the only possible LCA-compatible representation. Again, pronouns raise similar considerations; we could simply extend the solution offered for proper names and say that pronouns are not dominated by a single nonterminal node, hence can safely occur as complements of heads. Notice that this solution would not in principle distinguish clitics from stressed pronouns; there is no obvious reason why the X-bar structure they project would be distinct.[45]

Prima facie, then, there would be no reason to assume that a structure like (92) ever plays a role in syntax. In what follows I will show that a structure like (92) merging two heads is empirically relevant once a Dynamic Antisymmetry approach to movement is adopted. Let us consider the situation from a rather abstract point of view. If (92) is admissible, within a Dynamic Antisymmetry approach we expect such a point of symmetry to be neutralized by movement. I suggest that clitic movement in Romance is precisely such a case. More explicitly, I suggest that clitics are obligatorily displaced to neutralize the point of symmetry they constitute with the head they are sister to. Indeed, a connection between linearization (the LCA) and movement of clitics has been explicitly noted by Chomsky (1995, 337). This apparent convergence requires a brief comment, to avoid confusion. As illustrated here in chapter 1, Chomsky (1995) regards movement as merely a device to wipe out uninterpretable features at LF (see Chomsky 1995, 278; also see Chomsky 1998, 1999, 2000). In other words, in this view movement is a morphology-driven phenomenon. In fact, the connection between movement and linearization is never direct, in Chomsky's view. Movement is always to be regarded as a morphologically driven phenomenon even in the case under discussion. Simply, Chomsky recognizes that in this specific case the LCA can be weakened to let structures like (92) be generated, provided that movement displaces the clitic.[46] By no means, however, is movement forced by linearization in Chomsky's system; rather, linearization in (92) is possible because movement has intervened for independent reasons. Within a Dynamic Antisymmetry approach, instead, movement is triggered just by the necessity of linearizing items. In fact, under Dynamic Antisymmetry cliticization is just one aspect of a much more general

phenomenon of neutralizing points of symmetry for the sake of linearization at PF. Let us now turn to exploring an empirical domain, largely
using data taken from Italian and northern Italian dialects.

3.4.2 Remarks on Italian Clitics

Italian has a rich and complex system of clitics whose typology and
structure are a matter of debate (see the pioneering work by Burzio
(1986); for a general review see Renzi 1990 and references cited there). A
general partition can be made by observing that there are inflected and
uninflected clitics. Thus, along with uninflected clitics such as *ne* 'of it', *ci*
'there', and *lo* (a propredicative element),[47] Italian has fully inflected third
person accusative pronominal clitics like these:

(93) a. lo (masc. sg.)
    b. la (fem. sg.)
    c. li (masc. pl.)
    d. le (fem. pl.)

All these elements move overtly, yielding the typical proclitic constructions illustrated in (94).[48] For the sake of simplicity, let us focus on a
classic contrast in Italian syntax between clitic and stressed pronouns.

(94) a. Gianni la fotografa.
       Gianni her-photographs
    b. Gianni fotografa   lei.
       Gianni photographs her

A Dynamic Antisymmetry approach to such cases would force us to
assume that *lei* projects more structure than *la*; hence, no point of symmetry is created with the verbal head *fotografa*, and *lei* is not required to
move. How can we independently prove that? Two potentially available
explanations must be excluded. First, we cannot rely on any difference
between the two pronouns with respect to thematic information. If any-
thing, they should share the same thematic information; that is, they
project no argumental structure at all. Second, we cannot immediately
rely on the differing morphological status of *lei* and *la* to assign more
structure to the former. This is not to say that *lei* and *la* do not display
complex morphological information; simply, it is not immediately obvious
how this is relevant to distinguishing the two from an X-bar-theoretical
point of view, since they are both inflected with respect to number and
gender. I will not pursue this line further.[49]

What kind of evidence can we then seek to support the hypothesis that *lei* is associated with more structure than *la*? Since we can rely neither on the occurrence of any argument within a pronoun's projection nor on morphological structure, we are led to explore the possibility that some nonargumental phrase occurs in the projection of stressed pronouns that cannot cooccur with clitics. Relevant data are found in northern Italian dialects.

Pavese has the typical rich clitic system of northern Italian dialects (see Poletto 1993, Manzini and Savoia, forthcoming, and references cited there). In addition to clitics it has stressed pronominal variants. For example, *l'* is the clitic form of the tonic *lu* ([ly]; third person masc. sg.).

(95) a. Ho   vist lu.
         have.1SG seen him
         'I have seen him.'
     b. L'ho   vist.
         him.CL-have.1SG seen
         'I have seen him.'

The stressed variant *lu* can be preceded by a locative monosyllabic word *lì* 'there', as in (96a); notably, *lì* is not a clitic itself, as (96b–c) show.

(96) a. Ho   vist lì lu.
         have.1SG seen LÌ him
         'I have seen that person.'
     b. Vo   lì.
         go.1SG there
         'I go there.'
     c. *Lì   vo.
         there go.1SG

It is important to notice that the locative element *lì* does not introduce any locative meaning into the sentence; in fact, it just plays the role of a deictic, expressed by *that* in the English translation of (96a). Putting all these facts together, we can construct the relevant piece of evidence to support our argument. The locative element *lì* cannot cooccur with the clitic pronoun.

(97) *L'ho   vist lì.
         him.CL-have.1SG seen there

Some care is needed in judging (97). The sentence is grammatical if interpreted as 'I saw him there'; what is relevant here is that it cannot be regarded as the clitic counterpart of (96a) where no locative meaning is present. In fact, one can even combine the two *li*.

(98) Ho   vist li lu   li.
      have.1SG seen there-him there
      'I saw him there.'

All in all, these facts suggest that *li* belongs to the phrase headed by *lu* and hence that *lu* has a complex structure that is not shared by the clitic. As a first approximation, then, the structures underlying (95b) and (96a) can be represented as (99a) and (99b), respectively.

(99) a.

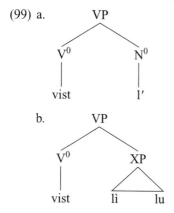

The reason why the clitic *l'* moves, then, is this: *l'* is a head; hence, (98a) is a point of symmetry and *l'* must move to neutralize it, as predicted by Dynamic Antisymmetry. Now, what is the internal structure of the XP? This phrase contains a nominal element *lu* and a locative element *li*. The latter can occur as a predicate in a copular sentence like (100).

(100) Al Nani l'è   li.
       the Nani SUBJ.CL-is there
       'Nani is there.'

A reasonable analysis of (99b), then, would state that these two elements, nominal *lu* and predicative *li*, are linked by a predicative relation. Since the minimal structure containing a predicative linking is a bare small clause, we can express the syntactic relation formed when the subject *lu* and the predicate *li* are merged as follows:

(101)   SC

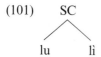

This is a typical point of symmetry, which needs to be neutralized. Notice that no linear order is specified in (101); now, since the observable linear order of *lu* and *lì* is precisely *lu lì*, it must be the case that the bare small clause is a complement of an abstract functional head (say, F^0), which provides a landing site for *lì*. Thus, this point of symmetry is neutralized by moving *lì* to adjoin to FP.[50] As for the status of *lì*, it is not unreasonable to assume that it has the same X-bar status as *lu* (i.e., it is itself a full phrase); in fact, unlike clitics, it does not move (96b), and it constitutes a point of symmetry with *lu*. If this were not so, it would be hard to explain these two facts in a natural way.

The existence of an abstract head occurring with stressed pronouns can be supported independently by relying on the semantic properties of these elements. A well-known general property of clitics is that, unlike stressed elements, they cannot be focalized. Let me put it in a very simple form. What is a proper answer to a question like (102)?

(102) Chi hai   visto?
     who have.2SG seen
     'Who did you see?'

One possibility is (103a); the clitic equivalent (103b) is not a proper answer, although it is perfectly grammatical.

(103) a. Ho   visto lui.
       have.1SG seen him
       'I saw him.'
    b. L'ho   visto.
       him.CL-have.1SG seen
       'I saw him.'

How is focus encoded in syntax? If we look at the domain of clause structure, focus appears to be implemented by a functional head within the left periphery, namely, by a head F^0 in the C^0 complex (see Rizzi 1997). The null hypothesis is that focus is implemented by a head in the nominal domain as well (see Giusti and Volchanova 1999 for a detailed discussion of focus in the domain of noun phrases; see also Longobardi 1994, Chierchia 1993, and references cited there for general discussion of the role of D^0). As a first approximation, then, let focus be syncretically represented within the left periphery of the noun phrase in the D^0 system.

(104)

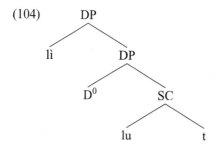

All in all, the presence of D^0 with *lu* is indirectly supported by the occurrence of the predicative element *lì*. A Dynamic Antisymmetry analysis of clitic movement is tenable and consistent with the analysis of why stressed pronouns do not move: stressed pronouns are associated with too much structure to yield a point of symmetry; clitics are heads.[51,52]

3.5   Concluding Remarks

To summarize this chapter illustrating some applications of Dynamic Antisymmetry: We first considered the potential points of symmetry generated by a slightly revised version of Merge (namely, (1a–c), repeated here as (105a–c)), from an abstract point of view.

(105) a.   XP   b.   XP   c.   XP

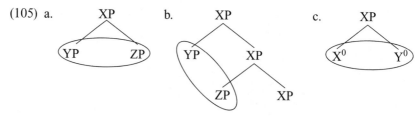

These three abstract possibilities have indeed turned out to be empirically relevant: each structure has been associated with a specific instance of movement triggered by the necessity of neutralizing the corresponding point of symmetry. (Moreover, note that the cases examined here cover the typology of movement exhaustively with respect to both the A/Ā distinction (sections 3.2.1 and 3.2.2, respectively)[53] and the X^0/XP distinction (sections 3.4.2 and 3.2.1–3.3.2, respectively).)[54]

The first case, (105a), merging two maximal projections, has been associated with the syntax of small clauses in copular constructions. We have seen that the two "mirror" variants stemming from small clauses with predicative nominals—canonical and inverse copular constructions—can be accounted for naturally by assuming that movement is required to neutralize the point of symmetry constituted by the small clause. Support for this analysis comes from comparing the syntax of copular constructions and *believe*-type verbs, which shows that "small clauses" require a finer-grained taxonomy including at least bare small clauses (with the copula) and more articulated constructions (with *believe*-type verbs).

The second case, (105b), involving multiple-spec constructions, has turned out to be relevant to explaining some core properties of *wh*-movement (including *do*-support, embedded *wh*-constructions, and locality effects). We have seen that Merge can stack more than one adjunct/specifier provided either that there are sufficient heads whose specifier each "extra" phrase can be moved to or that at most one specifier/adjunct is overtly realized. In fact, from analyzing agreement phenomena in Italian inverse copular constructions, we have concluded that if one of the phrases is base-generated as an empty category (specifically, *pro*), the multiple-spec construction can be maintained without involving movement. This reinforces the hypothesis that movement is triggered by the PF requirement to linearize words: if one of the poles constituting the point of symmetry is inherently phonologically empty, there is no need to replace it by a trace—hence, no need to move it.

The third case, (105c), has been associated with the syntax of clitics. More specifically, we have noted that clitics and stressed pronouns in northern Italian dialects share an important property: neither projects any thematic relation. However, only clitics move. By exploring the distribution of propredicative elements with stressed pronouns, we determined that this fact is related to the fact that an abstract functional head occurs with stressed pronouns.

As noted in chapters 1 and 2, the conjecture that lies at the heart of Dynamic Antisymmetry—that movement is triggered to neutralize points of symmetry—is too powerful to allow all its consequences to be checked in one work. Movement involves many varied domains of grammar, potentially all domains of syntax. My limited goal here has been to suggest that such a hypothesis can offer a different perspective on two central aspects of the syntax of natural languages, movement and phrase structure, suggesting that the former is derivative from the latter. Still, many questions remain. One major example is passive: can Dynamic Antisymmetry account for passivization? I have no immediate answer here. Another question is, does Dynamic Antisymmetry predict head chains (e.g., V^0-to-I^0 and V^0-to-C^0 movement)? This can only be a topic for future research.

Nevertheless, before concluding I would like to make a few more general observations concerning the way to look at movement from a Dynamic Antisymmetry perspective. More generally, in the final chapter I will speculate on a few general consequences that regarding movement as a symmetry-breaking phenomenon has for the overall design of grammar.

Chapter 4
Some Consequences and Speculations

In this book movement has been interpreted in a nonstandard way, while preserving the central minimalist thesis that there are only two interface levels (PF and LF) and that all principles must be expressed at one or the other of them. The difference between the standard theory and the theory proposed here is that the relevant level is PF, rather than LF.

In fact, movement can be regarded as a function of phrase structure geometry rather than morphology. Specifically, movement is a symmetry-breaking phenomenon, given the proper metric based on c-command and positing that the LCA is strictly a PF requirement. Movement is a blind operation that applies to the output of Merge, adjusting those structures that are not compatible with linearization. If this analysis proves correct, then two apparently unrelated major properties of all (and only) human languages—namely, movement and phrase structure—can be regarded as aspects of a single phenomenon: the linearization of words at PF. Indeed, reducing syntactic phenomena to configurational facts is not an isolated effort in generative grammar. At least two other major domains of syntax have been tentatively reduced to computation over the geometry of phrase structure: locality (as proposed in Connectedness theory and much related work; see Kayne 1984, Pesetsky 1982, Longobardi 1985) and θ-role assignment in argument structure (see, e.g., Hale and Keyser 1993 and comments in Moro 1997b).[1]

As noted earlier, many questions and many constructions that I do not even attempt to consider here could and should be analyzed under a Dynamic Antisymmetry approach. In this final chapter I would only like to speculate on two questions that emerge from Dynamic Antisymmetry. It goes without saying that these are not the only questions the hypothesis raises and that I cannot answer them fully. However, they are representative of the research program that Dynamic Antisymmetry points to, and they offer hints for a general reflection on grammar. The two questions I will address are these:

(1) a. Are all movements explained by Dynamic Antisymmetry?
    b. Does Dynamic Antisymmetry allow parametric variation?

The first question is clearly a fundamental one. I have not addressed it explicitly here; instead, I have taken the first step of showing that paradigmatic cases of movement can be analyzed as symmetry-breaking phenomena (revealing for example the otherwise hidden symmetry-breaking nature of *wh*-movement and cliticization). Once Dynamic Antisymmetry is adopted for some cases of movement, the next natural step is to ask whether it can be adopted for *all* cases of movement. Although I cannot pursue this task here, it is interesting to explore (1a) from a general perspective and ask what its consequences might be. In fact, the question whether all movements can be regarded as symmetry-breaking phenomena has no unique logical answer. One possibility is to reason as follows.

The most general partition within the class of movements distinguishes between overt and covert movement. Covert movement was originally proposed in the late 1970s as a way to capture restrictions on quantifier interpretation (see May 1985, Huang 1982, Longobardi 1991, Chierchia and McConnell-Ginet 1990, Hornstein 1995, and references cited there). That covert movement exists was an empirical conclusion based on two facts. First, the scope of a quantifier can be computed as a function of its c-domain (i.e., the set of nodes c-commanded by the quantifier itself); second, from an interpretive point of view quantifiers and *wh*-phrases can both be regarded as operator-variable constructions. The innovative hypothesis then was that the legitimate scopal readings of quantifiers are predicted by assuming that quantifiers can move (raise) covertly to reach the proper c-domain, under the same restrictions as those holding for *wh*-phrases. Next, another conceptually distinct type of covert movement has been proposed within the generative framework at least since Chomsky 1986a and has played a crucial role in the theory of syntax since it was introduced—namely, the so-called expletive replacement hypothesis. Synthetically, the idea is that elements like *there* are semantically vacuous; they are "expletives" that are inserted in specific structural positions for morphological and/or predicational reasons (and associated with a full noun phrase in some other part of the structure). Prototypically, in a sentence like *There is a man in the room*, *there* is the expletive and *a man* is the associate noun phrase. Chomsky's central argument relies on the principle of Full Interpretation, which requires that at a certain level only legitimate objects can be visible. Since by definition expletives do not have semantic content, they are not legitimate objects at LF, where grammatical structures undergo interpretation. For this reason, it was proposed that *there* be wiped out by replacing it with the noun phrase it is associated with. Simplifying, it is as if *There is a man in the room* becomes *A man is in the room* at LF. A major consequence of the expletive replacement hypothesis is that the distribution of *there* can be traced to independent principles governing chain formation. The associate noun phrase moves covertly to replace *there*, creating a chain: if locality conditions on movement are not respected, then the sentence is ruled out. A third type of covert movement, originally proposed to account for certain facts regarding verb movement, was then introduced (see especially Chomsky 1995); this type involved head movement. Stemming from Pollock's (1989) influential analysis of clause structure, this proposal claimed that languages can differ with respect to whether the (inflected) verb moves to I^0 before or after Spell-Out, yielding dramatic word order effects regarding adverbs. More recently, however, several independent arguments have led to the conclusion that these facts can be interpreted in a different way, crucially not involving (covert) head movement (see Chomsky 1999, 2000; see also Brody 1999, Kayne 1999).[2]

Summarizing, three conceptually distinct classes of covert movement have been proposed (although only two are still assumed), related to (1) the interpretation of quantifiers (quantifier raising), (2) expletive replacement (the expletive replacement hypothesis), and (3) head movement (prototypically, verb movement). In what follows I will concentrate on quantifier raising only. Moreover, I will assume that the expletive replacement hypothesis is not empirically tenable (see Moro 1990, 1997b, chap. 2, and the appendix to this book for a synthetic illustration).

Let us now go back to question (1a). Assuming that overt movement can be reduced to a symmetry-breaking phenomenon, this question can be reformulated more explicitly: can Dynamic Antisymmetry be applied to *covert* movement of quantifiers? The answer is twofold. In fact, if movement is a symmetry-breaking phenomenon and antisymmetry is necessary as a PF condition on linearization, there are two logical possibilities.

The first—indeed, radical—possibility is that there is no covert movement at all. After linearization has successfully taken place at PF, there is no need for movement: all structures must already be LCA compatible. In fact, the LCA would not apply after Spell-Out, since linearization is not even defined at LF. Interestingly, the hypothesis that covert movement does not exist has been suggested on independent grounds by Kayne (1998, 13):

> I have argued that in a number of cases where covert movement had been postulated it is possible and advantageous to dispense with covert movement (including feature raising ...) and replace it with a combination of overt movements [footnote omitted]. The strongest interpretation of this conclusion is that the cases explicitly considered ... are typical, and that it is not accidental that those cases lend themselves to analysis in terms of overt movement. It is rather that U[niversal] G[rammar] leaves no choice: Scope must be expressed hierarchically [footnote omitted], there are no covert phrasal movements permitted by U[niversal] G[rammar], and neither can the effect of covert phrasal movement be achieved by feature raising. Scope reflects the interaction of merger and overt movement.

Such a radical departure from the standard view requires complex and detailed arguments that cannot be reproduced here. The interesting fact is that the absence of covert movement is independently predicted by such a strong interpretation of Dynamic Antisymmetry. However, as noted, this is not the only logical possibility.

The second option is this. Saying that movement is triggered by the necessity of neutralizing points of symmetry before Spell-Out is not logically equivalent to saying that movement is prohibited after Spell-Out. In fact, the central conjecture of Dynamic Antisymmetry—that movement is required to neutralize points of symmetry—is consistent with the view that covert movement exists, provided, however, that the following restriction is added: there can be no *obligatory* covert movement. Admitting the existence of obligatory covert movement would amount to saying that the necessity of linearizing phrases at PF is not the only phenomenon that drives movement, hence that there can also be *overt* movement that is not driven by the search for antisymmetry. The empirical force of Dynamic Antisymmetry itself would be substantially diminished. Let us assume, then, that covert movement exists and that it is optional— a logically less restrictive possibility than the previous one.[3] What consequences does this assumption have for our understanding of language? It has some interesting advantages. Once covert movement is restricted to quantifiers (i.e., once the expletive replacement hypothesis and covert head movement are abandoned), this view accounts for a major property of syntax, namely, that covert movement is never obligatory (see Chierchia and McConnell-Ginet 1990, Chierchia 1995, and references cited there for an exhaustive discussion of this topic). As a brief illustration, consider a simple sentence like *Three students wrote two theorems*. This sentence can mean either that there are three students such that they wrote two theorems each or that there are two theorems such that three students wrote them jointly. Simplifying somewhat, the two interpretations are associated with two distinct structures, respectively: one where *two theorems* moves to reach the scope of *three students* and one where *two theorems* does not move. This sentence, then, is ambiguous, and the optionality of movement is the structural correlate of this type of ambiguity. This is clearly a very simple case; indeed, the idea that quantifier raising is optional is based on several, and intricate, considerations. Again, I will simply refer to Chierchia 1995, 144ff., and references cited there for detailed discussion. What matters here is that if this conclusion concerning quantifiers is correct and if the expletive replacement hypothesis is abandoned, then the optionality of covert movement (hence the ambiguity of quantified expressions) naturally follows from the general premises of Dynamic Antisymmetry: such structures are necessarily ambiguous because nothing can force movement after Spell-Out.[4] Notice that if movement is interpreted as a morphological fact, as in the standard minimalist framework, the optionality of covert movement becomes problematic. More specifically, there is no obvious way to combine the hypothesis that quantifier raising is triggered by the necessity of deleting uninterpretable features and the fact that sentences involving quantifiers are ambiguous. Of course, one possibility would be to assume that the optionality of movement is directly expressed in the lexicon. A priori, there are only two logical possibilities here: either there are scope-related features that specify whether a quantifier must have wide or narrow scope or there are optionally occurring uninterpretable features that force a quantifier to move; of course, neither option can be immediately assumed.[5]

Let us now consider question (1b), whether Dynamic Antisymmetry allows parametric variation—that is, whether there is a plausible way to express crosslinguistic variations in movement within Dynamic Antisymmetry. First notice that, a priori, there is no obvious way to make the LCA itself sensitive to parametric differences: in particular, the LCA is incompatible with directionality parameters, as noted in chapter 2. Of course, Dynamic Antisymmetry inherits from the original LCA-based theory of antisymmetry the inability to appeal to directionality parameters. Nevertheless, the way Dynamic Antisymmetry is construed leaves some room for speculation concerning possible parametric variations. The argument is as follows.

The very notion of parameter has recently been rethought. From different points of view, Kayne (1994) and Chomsky (1995) agree that parameters cannot be stated in complex formats such as the traditional "head-first"/"head-last" instructions. Crucially, crosslinguistic variation must then be established within the lexicon, more specifically in the domain of functional heads, as suggested for example by Borer (1984).[6] Consider the typical case of the relative order of the object (O) and the verb head (V) in root sentences. All OV languages derive from the universal head-complement order, which is the only one compatible with phrase structure, under both Kayne's (1994) and Chomsky's (1995) theories.[7] Simplifying, in Chomsky's (1995) theory parametric variations depend on the "strength" of the features involved: [+strong] uninterpretable features on the verb, for example, require pre-Spell-Out movement in order to be deleted at PF (OV languages), whereas [−strong] uninterpretable features can, hence must, wait until LF is reached (VO languages).[8] If we maintain the assumptions that parametric variation is in fact a genuine lexical phenomenon and that there can be no directionality parameters, a Dynamic Antisymmetry–based comparative analysis could still be viable. How can this be? Speaking very generally at least two conceptual guidelines come to mind. As we have seen, within a Dynamic Antisymmetry approach movement is viewed as the necessity of neutralizing points of symmetry before Spell-Out. Two properties define a point of symmetry: first, it involves two elements belonging to the same category (i.e., either both heads or both nonheads) that c-command each other; second, the categories are both overt (otherwise, no movement is required to neutralize inconsistent linearization; but see section 3.4.1 and note 10 of this chapter for some critical observations). Correspondingly, then, one can think of crosslinguistic differences that bear on either the first or the second property. Let us consider the first one by reviewing a simple case. Analyzing *wh*-movement, we have seen that *do*-support is related to the fact that when the object is fronted, it constitutes a point of symmetry with the subject; hence, the object must raise further to neutralize the point of symmetry. The second movement is signaled by the occurrence of an extra functional head, *do*. In this case the point of symmetry is constituted by two full phrases, the subject and the *wh*-object. Speaking in rather simplistic terms, we can say that Dynamic Antisymmetry predicts that in a language where the subject is expressed by a clitic, or stays in a lower position within the IP system, *wh*-movement of the object will not create a point of symmetry; hence, the *wh*-object will not move to a higher projection.[9] Another possible crosslinguistic variation involves the second property. In section 3.3.2 on rightward agreement in Italian copular sentences, we saw that Dynamic Antisymmetry is sensitive to base-generated empty categories, in that if either element constituting a point of symmetry is base-generated as an empty category, then it is tolerated and does not force movement.[10] For example, if the subject in a given language can be expressed by an empty category, we would expect *do*-support phenomena to be less evident. More generally, in a Dynamic Antisymmetry framework it is reasonable to conjecture that movement will be more evident in those languages where the inventory of empty categories is smaller than in others, since the latter languages display fewer cases where movement should intervene to restore the LCA-incompatible structures generated by Merge.

All in all, even if a comparative theory based on Dynamic Antisymmetry is not even on the horizon, at least we can conclude (1) that Dynamic Antisymmetry is not in principle incompatible with a theory of parametric variation that regards parameters as inherently related to the lexicon and (2) that the lines of reasoning one would follow to pursue such a theory are, at least methodologically, not vague. In fact, both properties for which Dynamic Antisymmetry predicts crosslinguistic variation involve explicit, inherently lexical specifications, namely, the capacity to project (clitics) and phonological content (empty categories). The research program would then consist of inspecting the correlation between these two factors and movement.

Dynamic Antisymmetry raises many more questions than the minimal one approached here.[11] The major aim of this book has been simply to suggest a way to look at two apparently unrelated properties of human language—movement and phrase structure—in a unitary way. More specifically, the theory presented here suggests that movement is derivative from the geometry of phrase structure in the sense that it is a symmetry-breaking phenomenon. I will conclude here, sharing the opinion held by many that a theory's primary role is to allow us to ask the right questions, more than to ensure that we find the right answers.

Appendix

Elements of Copular Syntax

Copular sentences play an important role in showing the empirical and theoretical advantages of Dynamic Antisymmetry in a broad sense. As illustrated in section 3.1, on the one hand, they do not fit into the theory that considers movement as a way to delete uninterpretable features; on the other, they constitute a prototypical case where a point of symmetry needs to be neutralized. In this appendix I will synthetically illustrate the fundamental issues of the unified theory of copular constructions originally proposed in Moro 1988 and expanded in much subsequent work (see Moro 1997b for a comprehensive illustration).

The analysis of copular constructions of the type *DP copula DP* has yielded far-reaching consequences in many domains of grammar, including existential sentences, quasi-copular constructions, and unaccusative constructions; moreover, it has shed light on core issues of locality theory. This appendix will mainly concentrate on locality. The discussion has three parts: the first illustrates the empirical reasons that underlie the notion "inverse copular sentence"; the second supports a theory of locality based on two principles; and the third sketchily extends the core result to other domains. It goes without saying that only a fragment of selected pieces of evidence for the unified theory of copular sentences will be illustrated here.

The term *copula* does not have a unique reference in syntax.[1] In English, copular constructions are those in which *be* is the main verb.

(1) a. A picture of the wall is impressive.
    b. A picture of the wall is in the room.
    c. A picture of the wall is the cause of the riot.
    d. There is a picture of the wall in the room.

Examples (1a–c) show that the copula is used to connect a subject with a nonverbal predicate—an AP, a PP, or a DP, respectively. Example (1d) deserves special treatment, and we will return to it later. It is standardly assumed that *there* is an expletive of the subject, and the corresponding sentence is generally called an "existential" sentence. Languages differ greatly regarding what structure is exploited to allow such predicative links. In this appendix we will concentrate on copular sentences with predicative noun phrases and see what consequences a detailed analysis has for the overall design of grammar, in particular for locality theory.[2]

Copular sentences with predicative noun phrases (henceforth, *nominal copular sentences*) have been extensively explored in many studies, across languages, since the pioneering works by Ruwet (1975) and Longobardi (1983). To a first approximation, they can be described like transitive sentences, namely, as sequences of the type *DP V DP*. In fact, however, it has been shown that this straightforward association cannot be maintained. Many empirical tests show that in some cases the postcopular DP behaves like a preverbal subject. Let us concentrate on a simple kind of test, based on Italian cliticization phenomena. More specifically, we will test two types of cliticization: cliticization *of* a noun phrase and *from* a noun phrase. A simple transitive sentence of the type *DP V DP* yields the following paradigm:

(2) a. Alcune foto   del   muro rivelarono [la causa [della rivolta]].
       some   pictures of-the wall revealed   the cause of-the riot
    b. Alcune foto   del   muro la rivelarono t.
       some   pictures of-the wall it-revealed
    c. Alcune foto   del   muro ne rivelarono [la   causa t].
       some   photos of-the wall of-it-revealed the cause

Cliticization both of and from the postverbal noun phrase—(2b) and (2c), respectively—is admissible. An analogous test on the preverbal noun phrase, instead, would have yielded a strongly ungrammatical result; the well-known generalization emerges that cliticization of and from a preverbal subject is ruled out. These facts have been captured since early analyses of clause structure by assuming that the preverbal and postverbal noun phrases bear an asymmetric relation with respect to the verb they are arguments of under locality conditions governing movement. Let us assume the simplest representation of this asymmetry, shown in (3).

(3)

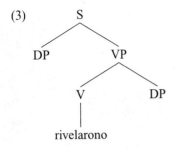

rivelarono

Of course, many other empirical phenomena support this asymmetry—for example, verb agreement, which reveals that verbal inflection is sensitive only to the features of the higher noun phrase. Indeed, one major contribution this approach makes to the theory of clause structure is that grammatical functions—subject, predicate, and the like—can be immediately derived from the configuration: thus, the subject of the predication is the "most prominent" noun phrase (here, DP), that is, the DP immediately dominated by the clausal node S; the object is the DP immediately dominated by the VP node; and the predicate is the VP itself. Accordingly, the whole cluster of phenomena yielding the differences between preverbal and postverbal DPs is generally called "subject-object asymmetries."

The asymmetric clause structure represented in (2) has generally been held to apply invariantly to all clauses of the type *DP V DP*. In principle, there seems to be no reason to restrict it to any particular subclass. However, once we consider nominal copular sentences, several anomalies arise. First consider the following sentences:

(4) a. Alcune foto   del   muro sono [la causa [della rivolta]].
       some pictures of-the wall are   the cause of-the riot
    b. Alcune foto   del   muro lo sono t.
       some pictures of-the wall   it-are
    c. Alcune foto   del   muro ne sono [la causa t].
       some pictures of-the wall of-it-are the cause

Prima facie, a nominal copular sentence embodies exactly the same asymmetric architecture as a transitive sentence (compare (4) with (2)). However, a sharp departure from this canonical behavior is clearly observable when the two DPs occurring with the copula in (4) are inverted.

(5) a. La causa della   rivolta sono [alcune foto   [del   muro]].
       the cause of-the riot   are   some pictures of-the wall

b. *La causa della rivolta lo sono t.
   the cause of-the riot   it-are
c. *La causa della rivolta ne sono [alcune foto   t].
   the cause of-the riot   of-it-are some   pictures

Both extraction of and from the postverbal noun phrase—(5b) and (5c), respectively—now yield an ungrammatical result, showing that the postverbal noun phrase behaves like a preverbal subject.[3] Indeed, many facts converge to the same surprising conclusion, including overt and covert movement in various languages. How can the data in (4) and (5) be accounted for in a unified way? The anomaly of copular sentences was resolved in Moro 1988 by relying on a raising analysis. Since Stowell 1978 copular sentences have been analyzed as expanded small clauses. The subject of a copular sentence is basically generated as the subject of a small clause and then raised to the subject position of the matrix verb, as in (6), on a par with passives of *believe*-type verbs (cf. *Alcune foto del muro sono ritenute la causa della rivolta* 'Some pictures of the wall are considered the cause of the riot').[4] This structure I referred to as the *canonical* copular sentence.

(6)   S   (canonical)

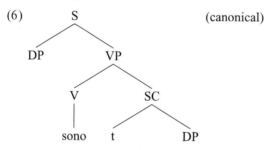

Notice that although this structure is more complicated than the one adopted for transitive sentences in (3), it cannot per se offer a unified analysis of the challenging data presented in (5). All we have done here is to increase the distance between the two noun phrases involved; we must still wonder why in only one case (i.e., (5)) the postverbal noun phrase behaves like a preverbal subject.

The solution to be proposed is crucially based on the hypothesis that along with the standard structure in (6), where the subject raises to preverbal position, there exists another structure that is its "mirror image"— namely, one where the predicate is raised to preverbal position and the subject is left in situ in postverbal position. A simplified representation is shown in (7); in Moro 1997b I called this the *inverse* copular sentence.

(7)   S   (inverse)

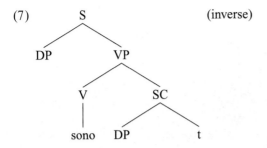

This structure enables us to capture the full range of data in a unified way. In particular, in inverse copular sentences the postverbal noun phrase is the subject of predication, a fact that allows us to trace the anomaly of (5) to the interaction of independent principles. In the rest of this appendix we will concentrate on this specific issue, namely, locality.[5]

Bearing structures (6) and (7) in mind, we can return to locality conditions as they relate to inverse copular sentences. Recall that inverse copular sentences play a role in arguing against a theory of movement as a way to delete uninterpretable features. On the one hand, this theory of movement requires the subject (of an inverse sentence) to move to delete the uninterpretable (nominative) Case features associated with it; on the other, all empirical tests show that movement of (and from) the subject of an inverse copular sentence yields strong ungrammatical results.[6] The question is why movement is impossible. Although I cannot go into a detailed analysis, I would like to show that the postverbal subject of an inverse copular sentence is in fact in the same syntactic environment as the preverbal subject of an embedded sentence as far as locality is concerned. For the sake of simplicity, I represent the two fragments as in (8).

(8) a.   C′   b.   V′

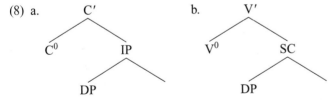

In both cases the subject is governed by a nonlexical head within a clause structure: the complementizer in (8a) and the copula in (8b), which is essentially the expression of the inflectional feature of the clause (much as in the original Aristotelian sense). Thus, under (some version of) the Subjacency Condition based on L-marking, the fact that the copula is inflectional, not lexical, would immediately exclude extraction *from* the noun phrase. L-marking is a local relation between a head and a full phrase: the head marks the full phrase according to the information specified in the lexicon. Prototypically, a head L-marks its complement; hence, V^0 L-marks the object, P^0 L-marks the noun phrase it precedes, and so on.[7] In general, the local relation that counts for L-marking is government.[8] In fact, neither C^0 nor V^0 is able to L-mark the lower DP. Although they govern it, they do not select it; hence, the DP counts as a barrier and blocks movement *from* the noun phrase.

However, the absence of L-marking cannot be regarded as the reason why movement *of* the noun phrase is not possible. In fact, movement of the noun phrase from this position is fully grammatical in canonical copular sentences. To explain why this is so, we can rely again on the fact that the subject of an inverse copular sentence is in the same syntactic environment as a preverbal subject—in other words, that (8a) and (8b) are essentially analogous as far as locality conditions are concerned. Consider the structural condition in which extraction of the preverbal subject is possible. Since Rizzi 1990 it has been assumed that such movement can take place by passing through the specifier position of a governing head and activating agreement on it;[9] in fact, if that position is already occupied (say, by a *wh*-phrase), extraction from preverbal position is impossible (e.g., *Who do you know t C^0 t represented Heaven in this way t?* vs. **Who do you know how C^0 t represented Heaven t?*). Thus, we can simply extend Rizzi's ECP-based analysis to copular sentences: if the specifier of the copula hosts the raised predicate, the lower subject cannot be extracted from the small clause for ECP reasons. This allows us to derive the facts simply mentioned in section 3.1 from principled reasons: the subject of an inverse sentence cannot be moved as a whole and nothing can be extracted from it, for ECP and Subjacency reasons, respectively.

Let us now concentrate on the solution proposed here: two distinct principles limit movement of and from the same noun phrase. Is a theory that invokes two principles acceptable? From a theoretical point of view, it is natural to try to reduce redundancy: why should two distinct principles block movement *of* and *from* the same DP? In what follows I would like to defend this two-principle theory of locality on empirical grounds. To do so, I will illustrate a natural extension of the inverse structure analysis to a different domain. To focus on a central contrast, consider the following case:

(9) a. Ci sono [alcune foto [del muro]] sopra il tavolo.
    there are some pictures of-the wall on the table
  b. *Ce le sono t sopra il tavolo.
    there they-are on the table

   c. Ce   ne   sono [alcune t] sopra il   tavolo.
        there of-them are   some   on   the table

The problem is this: the subject of the existential sentence in (9) is in situ in the small clause complement of the copula as the subject of an inverse copular sentence in (5). The situation is puzzling: extraction *of* the noun phrase in (9b) is indeed blocked, as it is in inverse copular sentences like (5b), but extraction *from* the noun phrase is possible, unlike in inverse copular sentences like (5c).[10] Whatever the explanation is, this fact is relevant for locality theory. The dissociation of the two processes of extraction of and from the same noun phrase strongly supports the proposed analysis invoking two principles: the very fact that just one can be selectively violated is hardly compatible with an analysis invoking a single principle. It remains of course to explain why the presence of *ci* has such a dramatic effect. The solution involves rethinking the role of *ci* (and its equivalents across languages), a process I will briefly summarize.

As noted earlier, there is a long-standing tradition of analyzing elements like preverbal *there* and its Italian counterpart *ci* as expletives of the subject (Jespersen 1924, Milsark 1977, Chomsky 1981, Burzio 1986). When raising does not take place, such an element is inserted to occupy the position that normally hosts the subject of predication. In Moro 1990 and 1997b I have proposed an alternative analysis based on the unified theory of copular sentences illustrated here. The core idea is that *there*, and its equivalents across languages, is to be analyzed not as a placeholder for the subject but as a placeholder for the predicate, and the associate sentence is to be analyzed as an instance of the much broader class of inverse copular sentences. Let us focus again on Italian. An existential sentence in this language and its counterpart in English are represented as shown in (10).

(10) a.

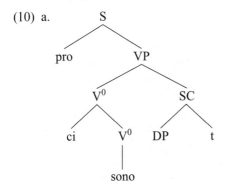

b.

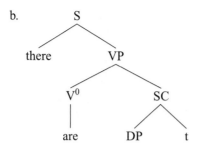

In this representation both *ci* and *there* are generated as predicate of the small clause and raised to preverbal position, as in (7). The difference between *there* and *ci* is that since the latter is a clitic, it does not occupy the topmost specifier position; as a first approximation, we can take it to be adjoined to V (and *pro* to be coindexed with it). The result obtained under the unified theory of copular constructions is clear: existential sentences are analyzed as particular instances of the broader class of inverse copular sentences. The advantages of this representation are illustrated very briefly here, on the basis of (11a–f); for full details, see Moro 1997b chapters 2 and 3.

(11) a. Ci   sono alcune foto   del   muro.
          there are   some pictures of-the wall
     b. *Alcune foto   del   muro sono.
          some   pictures of-the wall are
     c. *Ci   sono [bruciate molte foto]   dall'incendio.
          there are   burned   many pictures by-the fire
     d. Ci   sono molte foto   [bruciate dall'incendio].
          there are   many pictures burned   by-the fire
     e. *Ci   sono alcune foto   del   muro [la   causa della rivolta].
          there are   some pictures of-the wall   the cause of-the riot
     f. Alcune foto   del   muro sono [la   causa della rivolta].
          some   pictures of-the wall are   the cause of-the riot

If the existential sentence were the nonraising counterpart of the associated (canonical) sentence, it would be hard to capture the data in (11). Why should it be possible to omit the predicate in (11a) but not in (11b)? Why can *ci* not occur in passives (see (11c)) unless the object is exceptionally fronted to preverbal position within the VP as in (11d)? Why can a predicative noun phrase (like *la causa della rivolta*) not be present in the small clause when *ci* is inserted (compare (11e) with (11f))? All these questions (and others that I simply omit here)[11] can be answered straightforwardly if we adopt the representation in (10a) where *ci* is the raised predicate and the sentence is an inverse copular sentence. (11a) can lack a PP (or an AP) because a predicate is already present (namely, *ci*); by contrast, (11b) cannot lack a PP (or an AP) because if it does, the sentence lacks a predicate. *Ci* cannot occur with a passive VP in (11c) because a VP is not a suitable subject for a small clause. The "surprising" scrambling effect in (11d) is to be interpreted as the fact that *bruciate dall'incendio* plays the role of a reduced relative modifying *alcune foto del muro*, as in *Alcune foto del muro bruciate dall'incendio sono in vendita* 'Some pictures of the wall burned by the fire are for sale'. Finally, a predicative DP like *la causa della rivolta* cannot be present in (11e) because the predicate is *ci*, and crucially DPs, unlike AP/PPs, cannot occur as secondary predicates alone. In fact, the alternative analysis suggested here for *ci/there* forces us to analyze the PP/AP in the "coda" of an existential sentence as a secondary predicate rather than a main predicate of the small clause whereas the PP/AP of a canonical sentence must still be analyzed as the main predicate. Leaving a detailed analysis aside (see Rothstein 1983 on secondary predication), it is well known that DP contrasts with PP/AP with respect to the possibility of occurring as a secondary predicate (perhaps mediated by a small clause construction with a controlled *PRO* subject, as suggested in Chomsky 1981): for example, *John left the room angry* versus **John left the room a doctor*. For the same reason (11e) is ungrammatical. To further support the idea that the PP/AP in the coda of an existential sentence plays a different role than the PP/AP predicate of a canonical copular sentence, consider a contrast like this:

(12) a. A chi   sembra che molte persone siano [debitrici t]?
         to whom seems   that many persons are   indebted
         'To whom does it seem that many persons are indebted?'
     b. *A chi   sembra che ci   siano molte persone [debitrici t]?
         to whom seems   that there are   many persons indebted
         'To whom does it seem that there are many persons indebted?'

Extraction of the dative *a chi* 'to whom' yields an ungrammatical result only when *ci* is present, which is typical of extraction from adjuncts. Now, leaving aside the problematic issue of where the AP is inserted in the structure, there can hardly be any doubt that the two occurrences of that AP play different roles in the two sentences in (12).[12]

Assuming that the analysis of existential sentences as inverse copular sentences is correct, we can now go back to the two-principle theory of locality and reformulate the proper question: why should the raising of ci neutralize the violation of a locality condition? A reasonable answer comes from the way the Subjacency Condition is stated and from the fact that ci is a predicative element. For an argumental projection to count for Subjacency, it must not be L-marked. Recall that L-marking requires both government and selection. Now, the copula alone does not L-mark the subject of the small clause, because it governs but does not select it. However, once the predicative element ci is raised, it is not unreasonable that the complex head $[_{V^0}\ ci\ V^0]$ can perform the role of an L-marker. It governs the lower subject, as before, and now it selects it as well, albeit derivatively (i.e., via predicate-subject selection). Thus, extraction *from* the subject of an inverse sentence is grammatical, as in (10c). On the other hand, movement *of* the subject as in (10b) is still blocked, as in inverse copular sentences, since the specifier position that should be used to trigger agreement on the copula is already occupied by *pro*.[13] All in all, a theory of locality that invokes two distinct principles to explain why extraction of and from the subject of an inverse copular construction is impossible is now empirically justified.

To summarize: First, we considered empirical reasons to assume that inverse copular sentences are the "mirror image" of their canonical counterparts: in particular, we concentrated on inverse copular sentences and saw that neither movement of the subject nor extraction from the subject is allowed. Second, we saw an explanation for why both movements are blocked. We saw empirical and theoretical reasons to assume a theory of locality based on two principles (the ECP, as mediated by (spec-head) agreement, and Subjacency, as an effect of L-marking). The crucial piece of evidence came from existential sentences, which show that the two processes can be selectively banned. We interpreted the data by adopting the analysis of existential sentences as instances of inverse copular sentences, that is, by analyzing elements like *there/ci* as expletives of the predicate rather than the subject.

I would like to conclude this brief appendix by addressing a general point. We have seen that there are good empirical and theoretical reasons to conclude that inverse copular sentences are problematic for a theory that regards movement as a way to delete uninterpretable features. One point remains to be highlighted concerning the relevance of inverse copular sentences in the general system of grammar. In Moro 1997b, chaps. 3 and 4, I proposed that the class of clausal structures that involve raising of a predicative noun phrase includes more than just copular sentences:

namely, unaccusative constructions and sentences of the type *It seems CP*. As just one example of how the analysis can be extended, consider a sentence like *It seems that John left*. In the theory proposed in Moro 1997b its structure is as shown in (13a) rather than the usual one where the CP is the complement of *seem*, as in (13b).

(13) a.

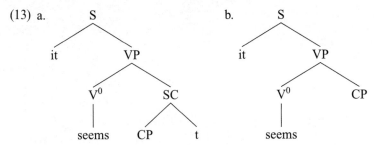

Notice that there is independent evidence that inverse structures with clausal subjects exist. Consider a sentence like *It's that John left*: given that the CP can surely not be analyzed as a predicate, the only other possibility is to consider it as a subject and the element *it* as a propredicative element, as in (14) (cf. *The interesting fact is that John left*, with raising of a full lexical predicate nominal, *the interesting fact*).

(14)

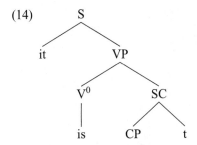

In every case, then—inverse copular sentences, existential sentences, *it seems* sentences (and unaccusative constructions)—we have evidence that the argument following the verb is not its complement but the subject of its complement, and the position traditionally reserved for subjects is instead occupied by a raised predicative noun phrase. Since each structure involves a small clause, an obvious topic for future research is to analyze these structures from a Dynamic Antisymmetry perspective.

Notes

Chapter 1

1. The empirical issue of displacement has been recognized at least since the 1940s and is sometimes referred to as the issue of "discontinuous constituents." For a critical and detailed survey of this matter see Graffi, to appear.

2. See in particular Chomsky 1995, sec. 4.7.1.

3. As far as I know, the structure of the languages of nonhuman species has not been exhaustively explored. However, if we limit ourselves to the language of primates, more specifically apes, there is overwhelming evidence that they lack syntax in any sense in which we apply this notion to human languages (see Terrace et al. 1979 and references cited there). Regarding the existence of movement in sign language, see Petronio and Lillo-Martin 1997.

4. It is well known that things are not so straightforward. In fact, the following contrast suggests that *who* might not have moved:

(i) a. *Who do you wonder which car fixed?
    b. ?Which car do you wonder who fixed?

We will come back to the ambiguous status of *wh*-movement of the subject in chapter 3.

5. The word *assignment* is used here merely as a descriptive label.

6. Interestingly, Case checking can no longer be assimilated to a criterion if the theory does not include Agr^0 heads, because there is no one-to-one relation between heads and maximal projections. Perhaps criteria could be reformulated in terms of correspondence between features in a head and maximal projections.

7. Minimality can also bear on the interaction between similar types of chains, as in Relativized Minimality (Rizzi 1990); according to Chomsky (1995), this interaction can be traced to economy of derivation.

8. The legibility conditions can be considered as manifestations of the general principle Full Interpretation, which sharply distinguishes artificial and natural languages; the discussion of Full Interpretation goes back at least to Chomsky 1986b.

9. Strictly speaking, the system must erase the uninterpretable feature on the target (see Chomsky 1995, 282ff.).

10. There may be differences both across and within languages about whether movement takes place before or after Spell-Out, depending on the "strength" of the feature involved. By definition, only strong features are visible at PF, so, if they must be erased, the process must take place before (or at) Spell-Out. If weak features must be erased, they can wait until LF is reached. Whether a certain feature is strong or weak varies across languages. The issue is complicated and still under debate, especially since within a derivational perspective Spell-Out can be regarded as a progressive process (the multiple Spell-Out hypothesis). I will not examine this issue here (but see Uriagereka 1999 for discussion of this and related matters).

11. It remains an open empirical question whether the locality conditions that apply to Agree are the same as those that apply to movement; in principle, this should be the case, since Agree subsumes the cases that were analyzed as feature movement in the earlier frameworks.

12. In fact, if a Dynamic Antisymmetry theory of movement is correct, uninterpretable features can only be affected by (long- and short-distance) Agree operations.

Chapter 2

1. In fact, two conceptually distinct hierarchical notions have been identified: dominance and the more restrictive notion of (c-)command. Using empirical arguments, Frank and Vijay-Shanker (1998) have proved that grammar can take c-command as a primitive notion, dispensing with the dominance relation.

2. See Graffi 1980 for a critical discussion of the relationship between X-bar theory and Greenberg's universals.

3. See Partee, Ter Meulen, and Wall 1990 for extensive illustration of this and related notions.

4. Terminology differs here. Some authors call this relation "connected." Many others, including Partee, Ter Meulen, and Wall (1990), call it "asymmetry"; for these authors, "antisymmetry" is the case whereby whenever $\langle x, y \rangle$ and $\langle y, x \rangle$ are in R, then $x = y$ (distinguishing between strong and weak linear orderings). I will follow Kayne's (1994) terminology.

5. Note that the term *linear* is not inherently related to the fact that words are physically put in line (sequence) with one another. "Being bigger than" is a (weak) linear ordering on a set of objects, but it has nothing to do with physical sequence.

6. Of course, not vice versa: given a sequence of terminals, one cannot immediately associate a unique hierarchy to it. In other words, there is no automatic procedure for assigning a hierarchy to a given sequence.

7. This version of c-command is not universally accepted in recent frameworks. In particular, by substituting *segment* for *category* in a definition like (16c), Chomsky (1995) adopts a version of c-command that allows multiple-spec constructions.

8. Interestingly, if either F or L immediately dominated a terminal node, (19) would be compatible with the LCA; the result, however, would be that the terminals contained in the "less complex" node would precede all the others in the linear order. For reasons I go into later, Kayne does not consider this possibility. Briefly, though: his theory essentially excludes such a situation because heads are not allowed to be specifiers.

9. Strictly speaking, Cinque's observation would leave the possibility open for clitics to be specifiers in case they are analyzed as having an intermediate status (i.e., as nonprojecting heads). I will not address this issue explicitly here; on the representation of clitics (within an LCA framework), see section 3.4.

10. Recall that (22) is just one possible representation (in fact, one that resembles the familiar one for languages like English) of four different orientations of equivalent trees. What matters here is only the hierarchical relation, since the linear order is automatically given under d.

11. Regarding the invisibility of traces, see Kayne 1994, 133, n. 3, and Chomsky 1995, 337. I will disregard the obvious problems posed by well-known phenomena such as *wanna*-contraction, simply assuming that contraction is blocked if the order is (locally) undecided.

Chapter 3

1. Antisymmetry applies below the word level as well (see Kayne 1994, 38–41). I will not consider this issue here.

2. *Well-formed tree* is intended here as a short expression for *tree whose terminal nodes constitute a linear ordering under d.*

3. I say "basic" because, of course, there can be infinitely many points of symmetry depending on the number of poles that constitute them—for example, adjunction of seven maximal projections in (1b). Nevertheless, all types can be reduced to this threefold taxonomy, which is itself not further reducible. In other words, Dynamic Antisymmetry is not imposing any limit to recursive application of the basic operation Merge. This recalls Chomsky's observation that "[t]he restriction to a single specifier is also questionable: rather, we would expect first Merge, second Merge, and so on, with no stipulated limit" (Chomsky 2000, 126).

4. Notice that the construction resulting from adjunction of a head to a head is irrelevant here, although possible; such adjunction would not constitute a point of symmetry, since the adjoined head would not be c-commanded by the other head. Multiple head adjunction, instead, would be a potential source of symmetry. We will not consider this type of construction here since it will involve exploration of (Dynamic) Antisymmetry below the word level. On head adjunction, see Kayne 1994, sec. 3.2; also see note 45 here.

5. Of course, it can play the role of an argument, but not all arguments can play the role of clauses. As for the notion of clause/sentence, I will not explicitly define "clause" here, assuming that some intuitive notion will be sufficient. In fact, a

formal definition of clause would take us too far; this can hardly be doubted. Graffi (1991), for example, reports more than 230 different definitions (this number is based on Ries's (1931) and Seidel's (1935) lists).

6. To avoid possible confusion, notice that this version of the split-Infl hypothesis is independent of Pollock's (1989) analysis (see also Belletti 1990 and references cited there). Despite the similar symbols they employ, the two theories are unrelated. In fact, the essential proposal made in Moro 1988 was to allow predicative raising to preverbal position, then called specifier of TP. The analysis of small clauses as AgrPs was also proposed by Kayne (1985) and adopted by Chomsky (1993, 1995); in the latter case it was related to Pollock's (1989) theory.

7. A similar case from Russian was noted by Jespersen (1924, 120).

(i) a. Dom nov.
       house new $(-\text{AGR})$
       'The house is new.'
    b. Dom nov-yj
       house new $(+\text{AGR})$
       'a/the new house'

However, this example might be problematic, since one cannot rule out that *nov* has a null agreement morpheme; see Pereltsvaig 1999 for a detailed discussion of (short) adjectives in Russian. In general, the crosslinguistic extent of this phenomenon and its correlation with Case assignment should be studied carefully; here this brief note will have to suffice. Special thanks to Lidia Lonzi for discussing the relevance of this case.

8. Of course, technically one can always assume that an Agr^0 head is present as a "null" Agr^0 even where no overt agreement is found. I will not adopt this solution, though; to do so would be ad hoc and (perhaps more importantly) incompatible with the case where agreement can be overt, as in the German examples in (8).

9. An alternative is available that takes advantage of the formal solution to the problem of representing adjunction within the definition of Merge. As indicated in condition (10b), the label of a constituent K can be complex, provided, again, that no information is added; specifically, the label of an adjunct structure is the ordered pair of the projecting elements (i.e., $\langle \alpha, \alpha \rangle$). It seems reasonable to assume that Merge allows a further combination, with the resulting label shown in (i).

(i) $K = \{\langle \alpha, \beta \rangle, \{\alpha, \beta\}\}$

This is also a formally acceptable option. Crucially, it does not conflict with the essential property of Merge, namely, not introducing extra information, specifically extra features of a constituent different from α and β. The format of this Merge output might seem to generate ambiguity, since from a purely formal point of view the mirror option, where the ordered pair constituting the label is inverse (i.e., $\langle \beta, \alpha \rangle$), is also possible. This problem can be solved by assuming that the label given in (i) is intended to be the short form of the more articulated one given in (ii).

(ii) $\{\{\alpha, \{\alpha, \beta\}\}, \{\beta, \{\alpha, \beta\}\}$

In this case the output is totally neutral with respect to α and β, and, crucially, the essential requirement that Merge not introduce new information is preserved. (I am indebted to James Higginbotham for extensive discussion on this topic).

10. Again, modulo the number of elements constituting the point of symmetry; see note 3.

11. I am not considering "free riders" here; this notion has been abandoned in more recent versions of the minimalist framework.

12. I will come back to the interpretation of small clauses in a weak antisymmetry approach.

13. More generally, the minimalist theory of movement does not seem to account immediately for the existence of alternative possibilities (for a given numeration), such as Italian "inverted subject" constructions and "preverbal subject" constructions (see Burzio 1986 for the standard analysis, and Belletti 1999, Longobardi 1999 for more recent proposals). Consider for example unaccusative constructions (whether or not they involve small clauses on a par with inverse copular constructions as proposed in Moro 1997b, chap. 4).

(i) a. Io arrivo t.
       I arrive
   b. Arrivo io.
       arrive I

If uninterpretable features of the nominative pronoun *io* 'I' can be deleted via Agree (or via expletive insertion), why should movement of the pronoun to preverbal position ever be possible?

Notice also that in a recent minimalist account, Case cannot even enter into Agree "since the probes do not manifest these features" (Chomsky 2000, 123); thus, the hypothesis that nominative Case features could be deleted by Agree, without involving movement, would be problematic even independently of the existence of two alternative strategies.

14. See Cinque 1999 and references cited there.

15. Notice that constituents like *in alcun modo* cannot follow the object in transitive constructions (ia) or the postverbal subject in either intransitive or unergative constructions (ib).

(i) a. *Maria non ha letto un libro in alcun modo.
        Maria not has read a   book in any   way
   b. *Non arriva/telefona   una ragazza in alcun modo.
        not arrives/telephones a   girl   in any   way

Again this reveals the exceptional status of the clausal complement of *believe*-type verbs, which include a much richer functional system than the complements of other types of verbs.

16. A residual, independent question is why inversion gives a considerably degraded result in the rich small clause complement of *believe*-type verbs.

(i) ?*Maria non ritiene   [la causa della rivolta F^0 ... Gianni t]].
    Maria not considers the cause of-the riot   Gianni

Descriptively, we can say that F^0 is not neutral with respect to the selection of the noun phrase in its specifier (perhaps derivatively, if F^0 is cliticized onto the matrix verb); that is, it requires it to be argumental rather than predicative. A comparative analysis suggests that *pro* might be involved (in fact, notice that the English equivalent of (i), *Mary doesn't consider the cause of the riot John*, is completely ungrammatical). Perhaps, *la causa della rivolta* has not been raised to the specifier of FP; this position could be occupied by *pro*, and *la causa della rivolta* might be in a lower specifier position. Moreover, the fact that *Gianni* is focused in (i) suggests that it might be in the same VP-internal position as focused subjects in Italian (see Belletti 1999, Longobardi 1999, and references cited there).

17. Notice that there is no way to interpret *which* as a(n autonomous) generalized quantifier in the sense of Barwise and Cooper (1981), that is, as a set-theoretical relation. Consider the following pair:

(i) a. Some boy runs.
    b. Which boy runs?

In fact, the interpretation of (ia) is that the intersection of the set of boys with the set of runners is not empty; there is no comparable way to interpret (ib).

18. For some English speakers, the plural is not acceptable in (37). I will disregard this problem here as it should not affect the argument.

19. The proper semantics of such a predicative linking cannot be explored here. I will simply rely on the fact that such a predicative relation is explicit in sentences like *Books are of this type*.

20. As for *of*'s role as a "hub" for raising either the subject or the predicate, notice that inversion in nonclausal constructions is not limited to noun phrases. For example, it is not unreasonable that the relation between the following sentences is similar to that between *this type of books* and *books of this type*:

(i) a. You are [t kind].
    b. It's [kind of [you t]].

In both cases there is a predicative relation between *you* (the subject) and *kind* (the predicate); thus, one can assume that such a predicative relation is implemented uniquely in both cases via a clausal constituent (a small clause). The different superficial result in (ib), involving *it*, is due to morphological restrictions.

21. The fact that the NP is represented on the left of the *wh*-phrase is irrelevant here, since the NP and *which* constitute a point of symmetry; that is, the two elements cannot be linearized.

22. Of course, I am not saying that a *wh*-phrase must necessarily be a predicate. In fact, the role of predicate (and its correlate, i.e., subject of predication) is not determined lexically for noun phrases (although it could be for pronouns, like uninflected *lo* in Italian). Rather, it is determined by syntax. There can be little doubt that one cannot decide a priori whether a noun phrase like [*the cause of the*

riot] can be a subject or a predicate. In fact, it can be both, depending on the syntactic configuration it occurs in and the phrase it occurs with. For example, consider the following cases:

(i) a. The cause of the riot is obvious.
    b. The cause of the riot is these pictures.
    c. The cause of the riot is the worst event I have ever been told of.
    d. The cause of the riot sleeps furiously.

Leaving a full analysis aside, it is clear that the grammatical role of the phrase [*the cause of the riot*] is not established at the lexical level; it is a predicate in (ib) but a subject in the other cases. Similarly, one could expect a *wh*-word like *what* to have a twofold role, depending on the syntactic configuration it is inserted in. Indeed, it would be problematic if this were *not* the case. Obvious examples are sentences like these:

(ii) a. What did John hit?
    b. What do you think this object is?
    c. What book did John read?

The *wh*-word *what* plays the role of argument in (iia) but the role of predicate in (iib). The difference between the proposed analysis and the standard one is that the role of predicate has been extended to instances such as (iic) where the *wh*-word does not occur alone with the copula but instead occurs within a noun phrase, specifically as a predicate of the NP (*book*).

23. Notice that there is a consistent semantics for the analysis that views *which* as a predicate. Suppose we have an LF structure of the form in (i) (where the copy of *which book* is visible).

(i) which book did [$_{IP}$ John read which book]

The semantics of (i) can be represented as follows. The IP component is interpreted as in (ii),

(ii) a. $\exists y$ read $(J, x) \wedge$ type (y, x)
    b. $\exists x$ read $(J, x) \wedge$ type (y, x)

where *J* refers to John and *type* is a two-place relation between types (of books) and books. One of the variables will be existentially closed (say, by existential closure); the other is left for the *wh*-operator in the specifier of CP to bind. Adopting a Hamblin-style semantics for questions, the *wh*-operator will turn (iia–b) into (iiia–b).

(iii) a. $\{p : \exists x[p = {}^{\wedge}\exists y$ read $(J, x) \wedge$ type $(y, x)]\}$
    b. $\{p : \exists y[p = {}^{\wedge}\exists x$ read $(J, x) \wedge$ type $(y, x)]\}$

This analysis says that there are essentially two ways of answering the question *Which book did John read?*: by naming one (or more) title(s), as in *John read the Divine Comedy, John read the Iliad, John read the Aleph*, or one (or more) type(s), as in *John read scientific essays, John read poems, John read science fiction books*.

    I am indebted to Gennaro Chierchia for having pointed out to me the semantic aspects of *wh*-phrases.

24. There are of course strings like *PP copula DP* (often referred to as "locative inversion"), but it can be shown that in such cases further movement has taken place to a position higher than IP, arguably a Top^0 position in Rizzi's (1997) sense. See Moro 1997b and references cited there; also see note 5 in the appendix for further remarks.

25. I will disregard whether Dutch is an SOV or SVO language. In fact, if we assume the LCA, this distinction can have only a rather superficial descriptive force. See chapter 4 for some speculation on this matter.

26. The last property argues in favor of the maximal-projection-like nature of clitics only if agreement is regarded as a spec-head relation and if specifiers must be maximal projections.

27. Interestingly, an exhaustive taxonomy of syntactic categories including bare small clauses (constituents that are not projected by a head) and ambiguous elements like *which* (heads that project without branching) can be descriptively captured in a natural way by adopting two abstract features: [±atomic] (i.e., single word) and [±projected] (i.e., being projected by a head). The abstract combination of these features gives the following pattern:

(i) a. $[+\text{at}, -\text{pr}] = X^0$
    b. $[-\text{at}, +\text{pr}] = XP$
    c. $[-\text{at}, -\text{pr}] = SC$
    d. $[+\text{at}, +\text{pr}] = $ *which, wat, …*

Prototypically, heads would be assigned $[+\text{at}, -\text{pr}]$, and maximal projections would be assigned the opposite value, $[-\text{at}, +\text{pr}]$. The other two possible value assignments appear to derive the residual phrasal categories in a quite natural way: elements like *which*, *wat*, and clitics are assigned $[+\text{at}, +\text{pr}]$ (i.e., they are simultaneously atomic and projected by heads); bare small clauses are assigned $[-\text{at}, -\text{pr}]$ (i.e., they are neither atomic nor projected by heads). Whether or not this descriptive taxonomy has substantive relevance cannot be discussed here.

28. I will uniformly translate *quali* by *which* and not by *what* (see Moro 1997b for a more detailed analysis).

29. These sentences with *di* are to be distinguished from sentences like (i).

(i) Cosa sai   di matematica?
    what know.2SG of mathematics
    'What do you know about mathematics?'

In fact, in this case *di matematica* appears to be a different construction, arguably a partitive phrase, as in *qualcosa di matematica* 'something of mathematics'; witness the possibility of using the clitic *ne* in (iib) but not in (iia).

(ii) a. *Cosa ne   hai   letto di libri?
           what of-them have.2SG read of books
     b. Cosa ne   sai   di matematica?
           what of-it know.2SG of mathematics
           'What do you know about mathematics?'

On *ne*, see Cinque 1991, Moro 1997b, and references cited there.

30. I am indebted to Luigi Rizzi for much helpful discussion on this issue. See Zamparelli 1995 for extensive discussion of the structural role of measure phrases. I will not attempt to analyze movement of *how/quanti* as a way of neutralizing a point of symmetry.

31. In Chomsky's (1995) approach, unlike in Kayne's (1994), the possibility of stacking more specifiers within a single maximal projection is maintained via the definition of c-command that relies on segments rather than categories. See also note 7 in chapter 2.

32. A detailed survey is not possible here. Among other works, see Rizzi 1990 regarding verb-second-like phenomena in Italian, Baauw 1998 for a detailed account of subject-verb inversion in Spanish within a Dynamic Antisymmetry framework, and Benincà and Poletto 1998 (see also Poletto, in press) regarding a northern Italian dialect with *do*-support phenomena.

33. I will not consider the analysis of objects as specifiers of more abstract entities involving Larsonian shells (see Larson 1988 and much subsequent work).

34. Diacritics are mine; Chomsky's example *What do you wonder who saw?* (1986a, 48, (105)) had no question mark.

35. Assuming the fine-grained analysis of the left periphery suggested by Rizzi (1997), C^0 might be $Focus^0$. This is not crucial here; however, a more articulated analysis will become relevant later in the argument.

36. In work in progress (see Moro 1999), I have analyzed *O* occurring in vocative Case (as in *I wonder, O Mary, where John went*) as an overt manifestation of (a feature/head of) C^0.

37. It is a well-known crosslinguistic fact that a matrix verb can select (overt) features of the head of the lower CP. For example, in Latin the C^0 of an embedded proposition governed by *timeo* 'to be afraid' can be either *ut* or *ne*, depending on whether the speaker hopes that the event expressed by the proposition happens or not.

(i) a. Timeo   ut veniat.
       fear.1SG UT come.3SG
       'I am afraid he is not coming.'

   b. Timeo   ne veniat.
       fear.1SG NE come.3SG
       'I am afraid he is coming.'

It is also well known that such selectional capacities are correlated with the distribution of empty categories in the Comp system. More explicitly, the very fact that a C^0 can be realized as a null category depends, in certain cases, on the presence of a verb selecting it in a specific configuration (see Kayne 1984, chap. 3). We see this in the following simple sentences from Italian:

(ii) a. *(Che) tu   parta è strano.
          that you leave is strange
       'That you are leaving is strange.'

   b. Credo   ?(che) tu   parta.
     I-believe   that you leave
     'I believe you are leaving.'
   c. Sono contento ?(che) tu   parta.
     I-am happy   that you leave
     'I am happy that you are leaving.'
   d. È ovvio   *(che) tu   parta.
     is obvious   that you leave
     'It is obvious that you are leaving.'

Among the conditions that rule this phenomenon (see Giorgi and Pianesi 1998 and references cited there) is surely this one: the embedded C^0 can be realized as an empty category if the clause is governed by a lexical head. This condition is met only in (iib) and (iic); in (iia) and (iid) either there is no head governing the CP or the head is not lexical (see Moro 1997b for an analysis of *obvious*-type constructions).

38. Notice that this is not equivalent to saying that IP cannot have adjuncts; rather, it means that any adjunct to IP cannot be the subject (it could well be an adverb, for example). Notice also that if this theory is correct, then the distribution of bare small clauses can be captured by saying that they can be complement of I^0 (see footnote 4, page 128) C^0, D^0, and P^0 (only), i.e., of functional heads only; for a unified analysis of functional heads see Emonds 1985.

39. Regarding the absence of *do*-support in the CP complement of *wonder*, we can reason as follows. In general, as noted in the discussion of (62), whether or not a complementizer is overtly realized is independent of issues of movement. Rather, in the case of root clauses it depends on their Force values. In fact, an overt complementizer like *if* also occurs in root nondeclarative sentences of the type *If they could only talk!* Notice also that *if*, unlike *that*, cannot be omitted (e.g., *I believe (that) John left* vs. *I wonder *(if) John left*); this can perhaps be used to support the idea that *if* is not governed by the matrix verb when it follows *wonder*, assuming that deletion must meet a strict locality condition (government).

40. The status of Op is presently under debate. Traditionally, Op has played an important role in understanding the structure of relative clauses. Recently, however, Kayne (1994) has suggested that relative clauses can be described without assuming the presence of Op (see also Bianchi 2000 for further refinements of the theory of relative clauses within the antisymmetry framework).

41. As far as I know, the unified theory of copular sentences adopted here yields the only case where verb agreement is determined by a predicate. On the relevance of verb agreement in the theory of clause structure, see Jespersen 1924; see also Graffi 1991, the appendix to Moro 1997b, and references cited there for a critical review of some proposals.

42. I have limited attention to *pro*. *PRO* warrants similar considerations, which I will not attempt to address here.

43. Notice that if one head projected as a head (yielding a two-segment category: X^0: $[_{X^0} X^0 Y^0]$), the structure would be compatible with the LCA, since Y^0 would be asymmetrically c-commanded by X^0.

44. The possibility of generalizing such a conclusion—that is, of claiming that there is no linear order if there is no movement—is challenging, but I will not attempt to do so here. Notice that this would imply rethinking the LCA as a function from the linear ordering of nonterminal nodes to a linear ordering defined on (nontrivial) chains rather than terminal nodes.

45. A second domain of inquiry where (92) might be relevant is word formation. Kayne (1994, sec. 4.5) applies the LCA to this domain also. Under this view the subword level is organized like the word level. In other words, hierarchy and the sequence of morphemes are not unrelated; rather, the same principle mapping asymmetric c-command into precedence holds with respect to the string of morphemes. For example, the verb *overturn* must be an instance of *over* adjoining to *turn*.

One might also explore the possibility that the order of morphemes in a word can be explained by Dynamic Antisymmetry. For example, the position of a morpheme like *auto* in *autopunizione* 'self-punishment' could be the result of neutralizing a point of symmetry at the word level. I will not attempt to pursue this hypothesis here.

46. Broekhuis (1995) has discussed and expanded this intuition, exploring head movement as a rescue operation.

47. For the sake of clarity, notice that *ci* and *lo* are homophonous with the first person plural accusative and third person singular accusative pronoun, respectively. For a detailed discussion of propredicative *lo* see Moro 1997b.

48. I will simply assume that clitics are not inherently associated to a full phrase. For a nonstandard analysis of clitics see Sportiche 1992 and references cited there.

49. Indeed, *lei* is underspecified with respect to Case, as it can occur in both nominative and accusative contexts whereas *la* cannot. Thus, if morphology mapped directly into structure, we would instead conclude the opposite, namely, that *la* is more complex. See Kayne 1999 for a syntactic interpretation of the differing morphological status of pronouns.

50. One could ask why the point of symmetry contained in the small clause cannot be neutralized by moving the pronominal element instead of the locative one. Interestingly, Tuscan dialects show the mirror-image pattern with phrases like *lu li*, inverting the order of Pavese: see Giannini 1995 for a detailed account.

51. This analysis suggests a further remark on the *li lu* type of construction. Let us consider the interpretation of *li*. This element has no locative meaning; it acts like a placeholder for a predicative element. This fact has a nontrivial connection with an independent domain. Indeed, it is directly reminiscent of the role of *there* in English *there*-sentences and of *ci* in the Italian equivalent. There is empirical evidence that both *there* and *ci* are propredicates that are raised from the position where predicates are generated (see Moro 1997b, chap. 2, and the appendix to this book). This process correlates with "desemanticization" of these elements, which lose their locative content. Thus, phrases like *li lu* with raising of the predicate *li* over the subject *lu* can be regarded, in a certain sense, as the nominal counterpart of the sentential predicative inversion structure involving raising of the predicative *there/ci* over its associate subject, also called "existential sentences."

52. The next step would be to analyze articles as raising from a lower bare small clause, on a par with *li*, unifying the analysis of articles and clitics; I will not pursue this line of reasoning here.

53. Only one instance of what is generally labeled A-movement is examined here, the other two being raising from infinitival contexts and movement to the specifier of IP of either the subject or the object DP out of the VP, in active and passive sentences, respectively. Although these are topics for future research rather than this book, I would like to add two observations with respect to A-movement. Regarding A-movement in cases like *John seems to leave*, Dynamic Antisymmetry would force us to assume that there is not enough space in the embedded clause to neutralize the point of symmetry constituted by the subject and IP (a small clause, as proposed in sec. 3.3), much as in the old S'-deletion analyses. In this respect *seem*-type verbs would contrast with *believe*-type verbs and *wonder*-type verbs, for which it is reasonable to assume a more complex CP layer in the embedded clause. Regarding raising from the specifier of VP position, a Dynamic Antisymmetry account would force us to go back to the analysis of auxiliaries as specifiers of VP typical of earlier theoretical frameworks (see in particular Emonds 1985, sec. 4.6, and references cited there). If so, then movement of the subject from the specifier of VP could well be regarded as a way to neutralize the point of symmetry constituted by the auxiliary and the subject—that is, a multiple-spec construction.

54. Strictly speaking, only one of the two possible instances of head movement has been illustrated here. So far Dynamic Antisymmetry does not appear to have obvious consequences for head-to-head movement (e.g., V^0-to-I^0 movement). Interestingly, the very existence of the latter type of head movement has been questioned in different frameworks (see, e.g., Kayne 1994, Chomsky 1995, Brody 1999). Whether or not this is accidental cannot be discussed here.

Chapter 4

1. If three major domains of syntax—namely, locality, argument structure, and movement—can be reduced to purely configurational factors, it would not be unreasonable to conjecture that all grammatical phenomena characterizing natural languages can be interpreted "geometrically" (and that we live in the best of all possible worlds).

2. Another type of head-to-head covert movement would be N^0-to-D^0 movement as proposed by Longobardi (1994); whether or not this hypothesis should be treated on a par with V^0-to-I^0 movement in the minimalist framework is a matter I cannot address here.

3. Notice that if this less restrictive interpretation of Dynamic Antisymmetry is adopted, the distinction between overt and covert movement becomes equivalent to the distinction between obligatory and optional movement, respectively.

4. In fact, this perspective allows covert movement to increase rather than diminish the amount of symmetry in the geometry of phrase structure: this seems to be a welcome fact, since many LF representations would include multiple Spell-Out constructions, such as those involving quantifier movement to the same c-domain of another quantifier.

5. For a critical analysis of quantifier raising in terms of feature checking, see Hornstein 1995.

6. Interestingly, Chomsky (1995, 235) views the lexicon in the "rather traditional sense: as a list of exceptions." This qualifies the lexicon as the proper place for crosslinguistic variation.

7. For development of this theory and a critical discussion concerning Dutch in particular, see Zwart 1997. Notice that in Kayne's theory there is no direct association between the SOV-like taxonomy (which is a descriptive apparatus) and the hypothesis that the X-bar schema is universally specifier-head-complement.

8. In Chomsky 1999, 2000, EPP-like features are introduced to account for movement. I will not consider this issue here, concentrating instead on the Dynamic Antisymmetry alternatives. See Donati and Tomaselli 1997a,b for critical discussion of this and related matters.

9. Clitic movement itself represents an interesting domain of analysis for Dynamic Antisymmetry; after all, clitics make a fragment of Italian an OV language.

10. Strictly speaking, this only applies to points of symmetry that are constituted by two full projections. For those constituted by two heads, movement is required anyway; see section 3.4.

11. Other general questions are these: Can Dynamic Antisymmetry predict why movement is universally upward within a derivational approach? If movement is a way to satisfy a PF requirement—namely, linearization—can we expect movement to be an alternative to other mechanisms at PF (such as intonational emphasis)? What are the theoretical consequences of Dynamic Antisymmetry for language acquisition? (For a Dynamic Antisymmetry approach to language acquisition, see Boeckx 1997) Again, such intricate issues cannot reasonably even be approached here.

Appendix

1. The literature on copular constructions is vast; in this appendix I will keep references to a minimum. For a brief history of the notion "copula," and for references, see the appendix of Moro 1997b; on the alleged radical ambiguity of the copula, also see note 2 here.

2. I will not follow Russell's point of view about the copula, namely, that "it is a disgrace to the human race that it has chosen the same word *is* for those two such entirely different ideas as predication and identity—a disgrace which a symbolic logical language of course remedies" (Russell 1919, 172). Rather, I will follow Jespersen's (1924) view that the copula should never be analyzed as a predicate of identity. In Moro 1988 I gave an empirical argument based on binding theory to support this position, which can be summarized as follows. Suppose the copula could cooccur with two DPs both of which are referential (in the sense of Geach (1962) and Higgins (1973)). A classic example would be (i).

(i) [DP The morning star] is [DP the evening star].

Binding theory shows that a pronoun contained in a predicative nominal cannot be bound by the clausal subject. This means that the latter is included in the local binding domain of the predicative nominal (witness contrasts like *John met/*is his cook* with *John* binding *his*; see Moro 1997b, sec. 1.4, on binding domains for predicative noun phrases). Now suppose we construct the following sentence, intending it to be an equative statement, that is, a sentence where neither DP is predicated of the other:

(ii) *[$_{DP}$ The morning star]$_i$ is [$_{DP}$ its$_i$ source of light].

Clearly, there is no way for the pronoun to be bound by the subject. On the other hand, if a predicate indicating identity—say, *equal to*—is inserted in the sentence, the result is different.

(iii) [$_{DP}$ The morning star]$_i$ is equal to [$_{DP}$ its$_i$ source of light].

Coreference is possible here just as in pure transitive constructions, which of course do not involve predicative nominals.

(iv) [$_{DP}$ The morning star]$_i$ lost [$_{DP}$ its$_i$ source of light].

Unlike (i), with a bare copula, (iii) is a genuine identity statement: neither DP is the predicate of the other, witness the fact that the local domain for binding is limited to the DP itself in each case. Notice also that if (i) is analyzed as an identity statement, the same should be said for the embedded sentence *S* in a case like (v), which does not contain the copula.

(v) I consider [$_S$[the morning star] [the evening star]].

Finally, it is important to notice that Russell unambiguously considered the copula to be a sign of identity when followed by a noun phrase and a sign of predication when followed by an adjective (the original examples were *Socrates is a man* and *Socrates is human*). Russell's statement to this effect has often been neglected or misquoted, it appears; had it not been, linguists referring to Russell's thought would always analyze nominal copular sentences as identity statements, which is clearly not the case. I would like to emphasize that what I am saying here is that identity is not predicated by the copula—equivalently, that one of the two noun phrases involved in a copular sentence always plays the role of a predicate. Whether or not the notion "identity" is suitable to explain the relation between the two noun phrases in a model-theoretic fashion is a different matter, one I will not pursue here.

3. One difference between copular and transitive sentences is that in the former the clitic associated with extraction of the noun phrase is uninflected. I will not analyze this fact here (but see Moro 1997b). Notice also that the verb agrees with the postverbal noun phrase; see section 3.3.2 for a discussion of this fact.

4. I am representing the copula here as V^0; a more correct representation would take it to be a direct manifestation of the I^0 system much as in the Aristotelian tradition (with suppletive roots for different values of tense, mood, and aspect). Notice also that the order of DPs within the small clause has only a denotational value here: since the small clause is a point of symmetry, the order is not fixed. Similar considerations hold throughout this appendix.

5. Of course, inverse copular sentences show up only when the predicate can occur in the same position as the subject (namely, when the predicate is a noun phrase), for bare morphological reasons. This type of structure is to be carefully distinguished from cases of "locative inversion." For example, Hoekstra and Mulder (1990) suggest that unaccusatives can be analyzed as "locative inversion" constructions where the specifier of IP is occupied by a PP (ia), on a par with copular constructions like (ib) (see Hoekstra and Mulder 1990, 28ff.).

(i) a. $[_{IP}[_{PP}$ In the room$]_i$ entered $[_{SC}$ a man $t_i]]$.
    b. $[_{IP}[_{PP}$ In the room$]_i$ was $[_{SC}$ a man $t_i]]$.

This analysis, which explicitly subsumes the analysis of *there*-sentences as inverse sentences given in Moro 1990 (cf. Hoekstra and Mulder 1990, 33ff.), cannot be maintained for empirical reasons. Consider the following examples:

(ii) a. $[_{DP}$ The cause of the riot$]_i$ is $[_{SC}$ a man $t_i]$.
    b. $[_{DP}$ The cause of the riot$]_i$ is/*are $[_{SC}$ John and Mary $t_i]$.
    c. $[_{PP}$ In the room$]_i$ is $[_{SC}$ a man $t_i]$.
    d. $[_{PP}$ In the room$]_i$ are/*is $[_{SC}$ John and Mary $t_i]$.

Assuming that agreement is invariantly established in the specifier of IP, it would be hard to assume that (ia) and (ib) instantiate the same type of structure. Rather, (ib) is an instance of the topic constructions that have been analyzed by Cinque (1990) and Rizzi (1997) as involving some portion of the scattered CP layer (and movement of the verb to a higher functional head). This would explain why the equivalent of (ib) in Italian involves a locative clitic *ci* that is not obligatory in an inverse copular construction.

(iii) a. $[_{IP}[_{PP}$ Nella stanza$]_i$ *(c') era $[_{SC}$ un uomo $t_i]]$.
        in-the room   there was   a   man
    b. $[_{IP}[_{DP}$ La causa della rivolta$]_i$ (*c') era $[_{SC}$ un uomo $t_i]]$.
        the cause of-the riot   there was   a   man

The status of *ci* with the copula is discussed later in the appendix; see also note 10. Regarding the lack of *ci* in Italian unaccusatives (but not in many northern Italian dialects; see Burzio 1986, Poletto 1993), see Moro 1997b.

6. Recall also that Agree cannot delete uninterpretable features here for reasons given in section 1.3.1.

7. There are various ways of implementing the notion of L-marking, relying for example on θ-relations (Chomsky 1986a) or selection (Cinque 1992). In Moro 1997b I adopt the latter version, as it appears to be empirically more adequate; thus, a head X^0 L-marks a phrase YP if and only if X^0 governs YP and X^0 selects YP. Interestingly enough, the notion of L-marking endures even in the minimalist framework. "Though varieties of government would be 'imperfections,' to be avoided if possible, the closer-to-primitive notion of L-marking should pass muster, hence also notions of barrier that are based on nothing more than L-marking" (Chomsky 2000, 117).

As for the class of phrases to which L-marking applies, notice that when the predicate is left in situ, extraction is fully grammatical even if there is no L-marking. Hence, we should regard L-marking (hence barrierhood) as a specific condition on argumental noun phrases, not on predicative ones, which behave like verb phrases, much as in the original definitions of the Subjacency Condition (see Roberts 1988 for a critical discussion).

8. For the sake of clarity, I will assume government to be a local c-command relation: a head governs its complement, the head of its complement, and the specifier of its complement. For a critical discussion of government see Giorgi and Longobardi 1991, Rizzi 1990, and Moro 1993.

9. Agreement then turns out to be the element that performs the "action at distance" that the ECP is about; and it has been proposed (Moro 1993) that it can be generalized to virtually all cases. In fact, this appears to be one possible implementation of a universal requirement that has long been recognized in generative grammar: "it is not unreasonable that U[niversal] G[rammar] should require that the presence of an empty category be signalled in some manner by elements that are overtly present" (Chomsky 1981, 251).

10. Selective effects on movement of and from the subject of existential sentences are detectable in English with quantifiers.

(i) a. There aren't [many pictures of [the wall]] in the room.
   b. There aren't [pictures of [many walls]] in the room.

The quantifier *many* cannot have scope over negation in (ia), although it can in (ib); that is, (ia) cannot mean that many pictures are such that they are not in the room, whereas (ib) can mean that many walls are such that there aren't many pictures of them in the room. Incidentally, the fact that in (ib) *many* can have wide scope would force one to reject the analysis of *there* as a scope marker proposed in Williams 1984. On the reason why *there* affects the copula like *ci*, see Moro 1997b, chap. 3.

11. Incidentally, it is possible to trace the distribution of predicative elements like *ci/there* to locality conditions on movement, as in the original standard analysis based on the expletive replacement hypothesis. The alternative proposal suggested here, however, appears to be empirically more advantageous since it can account for cases like (i) that resist the former analysis, as explicitly recognized in Chomsky 1995.

(i) *There seems a picture of the wall to be t t (on sale).

The ungrammaticality of (i) can be traced to the fact that the subject of an inverse copular construction cannot move; in other words, (i) is equivalent to *The cause of the riot seems a picture of the wall to be*.

12. The nonstandard analysis of *ci* offers interesting insight into the position of PP/AP in the coda of an existential sentence. Consider the following sentence:

(i) Un libro, lo leggo.
   a   book it-read.1SG
   'A book, I read it.'

This sentence is a topic construction (topic constructions in Italian being realized as clitic left dislocation (CLLD) constructions; see Cinque 1990 for a detailed discussion); in particular, *un libro* is in the specifier of TopP, and *lo* is the clitic associated with it. In Italian (i) can also be rendered as in (ii), which can perhaps be analyzed as a case of remnant movement of IP to the specifier of a further functional projection within the CP layer.

(ii) Lo leggo, un libro.
    it-read.1SG a book
    'I read it, a book.'

Thus, one can reasonably argue that the PP of an existential sentence like (iii) is in the specifier position of the same functional projection as *un libro* in (ii)—namely, the specifier of TopP, with further movement of IP to the specifier of a higher functional projection.

(iii) C'è   un gatto, in giardino.
     there is a cat   in garden

Interestingly, extraction from the noun phrase in CLLD constructions like (ii) yields the same type of contrast observed in (12) in the text, supporting the hypothesis that the AP/PP in the coda of an existential sentence corresponds to the XP of CLLD constructions such as (ii).

(iv) a. *Di chi   l'hai   visto [un ritratto t]?
        of whom it-have.2SG seen a   picture
    b. Di chi   hai   visto [un ritratto t]?
        of whom have.2SG seen a   picture

13. Interestingly, in Italian existential sentences agreement is not obligatory, as in (i).

(i) a. C'è   dei pezzi di muro.
       there is some pieces of wall
   b. Ci   sono dei pezzi di muro.
      there are some pieces of wall

It has been suggested (Moro 1997b, chap. 3) that the clitic status of *ci* is to be related, via movement, to the lack of a definiteness effect in Italian. When the subject is definite, agreement is obligatory, as in (ii).

(ii) a. *C'è   loro in giardino.
        there is they in garden
    b. Ci   sono loro in giardino.
        there are they in garden

This suggests that the subject has passed through to preverbal position in the course of the derivation, triggering agreement. Of course, this option is not available in English, since the counterpart of *ci*—namely, *there*—is not a clitic.

References

Abney, S. 1987. The English noun phrase in its sentential aspect. Doctoral dissertation, MIT.

Baauw, S. 1998. Subject verb inversion in Spanish *wh*-questions. In R. van Bezooijen and R. Kager, eds., *Linguistics in the Netherlands 1998*. Amsterdam: John Benjamins.

Baker, M. 1988. *Incorporation*. Chicago: University of Chicago Press.

Barwise, J., and R. Cooper. 1981. Generalized quantifiers and natural language. *Linguistics and Philosophy* 4, 159–219.

Belletti, A. 1990. *Generalized verb movement*. Turin: Rosenberg & Sellier.

Belletti, A. 1999. Inversion as focalization. In A. Hulke and J.-Y. Pollock, eds., *Inversion in Romance*. Oxford: Oxford University Press.

Benincà, P., and C. Poletto. 1998. A case of *do*-support in Romance. In *Working papers in linguistics 8.1*. Università di Venezia.

Bennis, H. 1986. *Gaps and dummies*. Dordrecht: Foris.

Bianchi, V. 2000. The raising analysis of relative clauses: A reply to Borsley. *Linguistic Inquiry* 31, 123–140.

Boeckx, C. 1997. Beyond small children's small clauses: Kids, Kayne and clause formation. Ms., University of Connecticut, Storrs.

Borer, H. 1984. *Parametric syntax*. Dordrecht: Foris.

Bowers, J. 1993. The syntax of predication. *Linguistic Inquiry* 24, 591–656.

Brody, M. 1999. Syntactic representation in Perfect Syntax. Ms., University College, London, and Linguistics Institute, HAS, Budapest.

Broekhuis, H. 1995. On heads and the Linear Correspondence Axiom. Ms., University of Amsterdam.

Burzio, L. 1986. *Italian syntax*. Dordrecht: Reidel.

Cardinaletti, A., and M. T. Guasti, eds. 1995. *Small clauses*. San Diego, Calif.: Academic Press.

Cardinaletti, A., and M. Starke. 1994. The typology of structural deficiency: On three grammatical classes. In *Working papers in linguistics 4*. Università di Venezia.

Carlson, G., and F. J. Pelletier. 1995. *The generic book*. Chicago: University of Chicago Press.

Chierchia, G. 1993. Reference to kinds twenty years later. Paper presented at "Events in Linguistics," Bar Ilan University, Tel Aviv.

Chierchia, G. 1995. *Dynamics of meaning*. Chicago: University of Chicago Press.

Chierchia, G., and S. McConnell-Ginet. 1990. *Meaning and grammar*. Cambridge, Mass.: MIT Press.

Chomsky, N. 1957. *Syntactic structures*. The Hague: Mouton.

Chomsky, N. 1981. *Lectures on government and binding*. Dordrecht: Foris.

Chomsky, N. 1986a. *Barriers*. Cambridge, Mass.: MIT Press.

Chomsky, N. 1986b. *Knowledge of language*. New York: Praeger.

Chomsky, N. 1993. A minimalist program for linguistic theory. In K. Hale and S. J. Keyser, eds. *The view from Building 20*. Cambridge, Mass.: MIT Press.

Chomsky, N. 1995. Categories and transformations. In *The Minimalist Program*. Cambridge, Mass.: MIT Press.

Chomsky, N. 1998. New horizons on the study of language. Ms., MIT.

Chomsky, N. 1999. Derivation by phase. Ms., MIT. [To appear in M. Kenstowicz, ed., *Ken Hale: A life in linguistics*. Cambridge, Mass.: MIT Press.]

Chomsky, N. 2000. Minimalist inquiries: The framework. In R. Martin, D. Michaels, and J. Uriagereka, eds., *Step by step*. Cambridge, Mass.: MIT Press.

Cinque, G. 1980. On extraction from NP in Italian. Journal of Italian Linguistics 5, 47–99.

Cinque, G. 1990. *Types of Ā-dependencies*. Cambridge, Mass.: MIT Press.

Cinque, G. 1991. Lo statuto categoriale del *ne* partitivo. In *Saggi di linguistica e di letteratura in memoria di Paolo Zolli*. Padua: Antenore.

Cinque, G. 1992. Functional projections and N movement within DP. Talk given at the XV GLOW Colloquium, Lisbon.

Cinque, G. 1995. The pseudo-relative and acc-*ing* constructions after verbs of perception. In *Italian syntax and Universal Grammar*. Cambridge: Cambridge University Press.

Cinque, G. 1996. The antisymmetric program: Theoretical and typological implications. *Journal of Linguistics* 32, 447–464.

Cinque, G. 1999. *Adverbs and functional heads: A cross-linguistic perspective*. Oxford: Oxford University Press.

Dikken, M. den. 1999. Predicate inversion in DP. In A. Alexiadou and C. Wilder, eds., *Studies on the determiner phrase*. Amsterdam: John Benjamins.

Donati, C. 1995. Il *que* relativo spagnolo. *Lingua e Stile* 30, 565–595.

Donati, C., and A. Tomaselli. 1997a. Language types and generative grammar: A review of some consequences of the universal VO hypothesis. In D. Beezman, D. LeBlanc, and H. van Riemsdijk, eds., *Right ward movement*. Amsterdam: John Benjamins.

Donati, C., and A. Tomaselli. 1997b. La sintassi del soggetto nel quadro minimalista. *Lingua e Stile* 32, 223–245.

Emonds, J. 1985. *A unified theory of syntactic categories*. Dordrecht: Foris.

Frank, R., and K. Vijay-Shanker. 1998. Primitive c-command. Ms., The Johns Hopkins University.

Geach, P. 1962. *Reference and generality*. Ithaca, N.Y.: Cornell University Press.

George, L. 1980. Analogical generalization in natural language syntax. Doctoral dissertation, MIT.

Giannini, S. 1995. Riferimenti deittici nel sistema dei pronomi personali: Appunti per una grammatica del Lucchese. *Archivio Glottologico Italiano* 80, I/II, 204–238.

Giorgi, A., and G. Longobardi. 1991. *The syntax of noun phrases*. Cambridge: Cambridge University Press.

Giorgi, A., and F. Pianesi. 1998. *Tense and aspect: From semantics to morphosyntax*. Oxford: Oxford University Press.

Giusti, G., and M.-D. Vulchanova. 1999. Fragments of Balkan nominal structure. In A. Alexiadou and C. Wilder, eds., *Studies on the determiner phrase*. Amsterdam: John Benjamins.

Graffi, G. 1980. Universali di Greenberg e grammatica generativa. *Lingua e Stile* 15, 371–387.

Graffi, G. 1991. *La sintassi tra Ottocento e Novecento*. Bologna: Il Mulino.

Graffi, G. 1997. Frasi complete e frasi ridotte. *Lingua e Stile* 32, 273–291.

Graffi, G. To appear. *History of syntax in the XIX and XX centuries*. Amsterdam: John Benjamins.

Greenberg, J. H., ed. 1963. *Universals of language*. Cambridge, Mass.: MIT Press.

Haegeman, L. 1990. Non-overt subjects in diary contexts. In J. Mascaró and M. Nespor, eds., *Grammar in progress*. Dordrecht: Foris.

Haegeman, L., and R. Zanuttini. 1991. Negative heads and the Negative Criterion. *The Linguistic Review* 8, 233–251.

Hale, K., and S. J. Keyser. 1993. On the argument structure and the lexical expression of syntactic relations. In K. Hale and S. J. Keyser, eds., *The view from Building 20: Essays in linguistics in honor of Sylvain Bromberger*. Cambridge, Mass.: MIT Press.

Higginbotham, J. 1983. Logical Form, binding, and nominals. *Linguistic Inquiry* 14, 395–420.

Higginbotham, J. 1990. Philosophy of language. In D. Osherson and H. Lasnik, eds., *An invitation to cognitive science*. Vol. 1, *Language*. Cambridge, Mass.: MIT Press.

Higgins, F. R. 1973. The pseudo-cleft construction in English. Doctoral dissertation, MIT. [Published 1979, New York: Garland.]

Hoekstra, T., and R. Mulder. 1990. Unergatives as copular verbs. *The Linguistic Review* 7, 1–79.

Hornstein, N. 1995. *Logical Form*. Oxford: Blackwell.

Huang, C.-T. J. 1982. Logical relations in Chinese and the theory of grammar. Doctoral dissertation, MIT.

Jespersen, O. 1924. *The philosophy of grammar*. London: Allen & Unwin.

Kayne, R. 1984. *Connectedness and binary branching*. Dordrecht: Foris.

Kayne, R. 1985. L'accord du participe passé en français et en italien. *Modèles Linguistiques* 7, 73–89.

Kayne, R. 1989. Null subjects and clitic climbing. In O. Jaeggli and K. Safir, eds., *The null subject parameter*. Dordrecht: Kluwer.

Kayne, R. 1994. *The antisymmetry of syntax*. Cambridge, Mass.: MIT Press.

Kayne, R. 1998. Overt vs. covert movement. *Syntax* 1, 128–191.

Kayne, R. 1999. The person morphemes. Ms., New York University.

Larson, R. 1988. On the double object construction. *Linguistic Inquiry* 19, 335–391.

Longobardi, G. 1983. Su alcune proprietà della sintassi e della forma logica delle frasi copulari. In *Sintassi e morfologia della lingua italiana d'uso: Teorie ed applicazioni descrittive*. Rome: Bulzoni.

Longobardi, G. 1985. Connectedness, scope, and c-command. *Linguistic Inquiry* 16, 163–192.

Longobardi, G. 1988. *Symmetry principles in syntax*. Padua: Clesp.

Longobardi, G. 1990. *Lezioni di sintassi generale e comparata*. Venice: Editoria Universitaria.

Longobardi, G. 1991. In defense of the correspondence hypothesis. In R. May and R. Huang, eds., *Logical structure and linguistic structure*. Dordrecht: Reidel.

Longobardi, G. 1994. Reference and proper names: A theory of N-movement in Syntax and Logical Form. *Linguistic Inquiry* 25, 609–665.

Longobardi, G. 1999. Different types of inverted subjects. Ms., Università di Trieste.

Manzini, M. R. 1983. Restructuring and reanalysis. Doctoral dissertation, MIT.

Manzini, M. R. 1992. *Locality*. Cambridge, Mass.: MIT Press.

Manzini, M. R., and L. Savoia. Forthcoming. *I dialetti italiani*. Bologna: Il Mulino.

May, R. 1985. *Logical Form*. Cambridge, Mass.: MIT Press.

Milsark, G. L. 1977. Toward an explanation of certain peculiarities in the existential construction in English. *Linguistic Analysis* 3, 1–30.

Moro, A. 1988. Per una teoria unificata delle frasi copulari. *Rivista di Grammatica Generativa* 13, 81–110.

Moro, A. 1990. *There*-raising: Principles across levels. Talk given at the XIII GLOW Colloquium, St. John's College, Cambridge.

Moro, A. 1993. Heads as antecedents: A brief history of the ECP. *Lingua e Stile* 28, 31–57.

Moro, A. 1997a. Dynamic Antisymmetry: Movement as a symmetry-breaking phenomenon. *Studia Linguistica* 51, 50–76.

Moro, A. 1997b. *The raising of predicates: Predicative noun phrases and the theory of clause structure.* Cambridge: Cambridge University Press.

Moro, A. 1999. Notes on vocative case. Talk given at the Incontro di Grammatica Generativa, Università di Siena.

Partee, B. H., A. ter Meulen, and R. E. Wall. 1990. *Mathematical methods in linguistics.* Dordrecht: Kluwer.

Pereltsvaig, A. 1999. Short and long adjectives in Russian. Ms., McGill University.

Pesetsky, D. 1982. Paths and categories. Doctoral dissertation, MIT.

Petronio, K., and D. Lillo-Martin. 1997. *Wh*-movement and the position of spec-CP: Evidence from American Sign Language. *Language* 73, 18–57.

Poletto, C. 1993. La sintassi del soggetto nei dialetti italiani settentrionali. *Quaderni Patavine di Linguistica*, Monografie 12. Padua: Unipress.

Poletto, C. In press. *The higher functional field: Evidence from the northern Italian dialects.* Oxford: Oxford University Press.

Pollock, J.-Y. 1989. Verb movement, Universal Grammar, and the structure of IP. *Linguistic Inquiry* 20, 365–424.

Reinhart, T. 1976. The syntax of anaphora. Doctoral dissertation, MIT.

Renzi, L., ed. 1990. *Grande grammatica italiana di consultazione*, vol. 1. Bologna: Il Mulino.

Riemsdijk, H. van. 1978. *A case study in syntactic markedness.* Lisse: Peter de Ridder Press. [Distributed by Foris, Dordrecht.]

Ries, J. 1931. *Was ist ein Satz? Ein Kritischer Versuch.* 2nd ed. Prague: Taussig & Taussig.

Rizzi, L. 1990. *Relativized Minimality.* Cambridge, Mass.: MIT Press.

Rizzi, L. 1996. Residual verb-second and the *Wh*-Criterion. Technical Reports in Formal and Computational Linguistics 2. Université de Genève.

Rizzi, L. 1997. The fine structure of Comp. In L. Haegeman, ed., *Elements of grammar.* Dordrecht: Kluwer.

Roberts, I. 1988. From rules to constraints. *Lingua e Stile* 23, 445–464.

Rothstein, S. 1983. The syntactic form of predication. Doctoral dissertation, MIT.

Russell, B. 1919. *The philosophy of mathematics.* London: Allen & Unwin.

Ruwet, N. 1975. Les phrases copulatives. In *Recherches linguistiques 3*, 143–191. Université de Paris-Vincennes.

Seidel, E. 1935. *Geschichte und Kritik der wichtigsten Satzdefinitionen*. Jena: Biedermann.

Sportiche, D. 1992. Clitic constructions. Ms., UCLA.

Stowell, T. 1978. What was there before *there* was there. In D. Farkas et al., eds., *Papers from the Fourteenth Regional Meeting, Chicago Linguistic Society*. Chicago Linguistic Society, University of Chicago.

Stowell, T. 1981. Origins of phrase structure. Doctoral dissertation, MIT.

Terrace, H. S., L. A. Petitto, R. J. Sanders, and T. G. Bever. 1979. Can an ape create a sentence? *Science* 206(4421), 891–902.

Uriagereka, J. 1999. Multiple Spell-Out. In S. D. Epstein and N. Hornstein, eds., *Working minimalism*. Cambridge, Mass.: MIT Press.

Williams, E. 1975. Small clauses in English. In J. Kimball, ed., *Syntax and semantics 4*. New York: Academic Press.

Williams, E. 1980. Predication. *Linguistic Inquiry* 11, 203–238.

Williams, E. 1984. *There*-insertion. *Linguistic Inquiry* 15, 131–153.

Zamparelli, R. 1995. Layers in the determiner phrase. Doctoral dissertation, University of Rochester.

Zwart, J.-W. 1997. Dutch is head-initial. *The Linguistic Review* 11, 377–406.

Index

Abney, S., 50
Adjuncts,
  in the antisymmetry theory, 23–25
  in existential sentences, 111
  and specifiers, 25 (*see also* Multiple-spec
    constructions)
Agreement,
  and predication, 35–36
  as relevant for locality theory, 108, 130n9
    (*see also* Rightward agreement)
Antisymmetry Theory,
  and the derivation of the X-bar theory,
    26–27
  different aspects of, 17
  as opposed to the traditional view, 16–17
    (*see also* LCA)

Baauw, S., 123n32
Baker, M., 9
Bare Output Conditions (BOC), 11, 13–14.
  See also Minimalism; Interfaces
Bare small clauses,
  abstract case as points of symmetry, 38–
    39
  as complements of the copula, 43
  as distinct from the complements of
    believe-type verbs, 43–48
  vs. IPs as the only predicational structures,
    71
  as selected by $I^0/C^0/P^0/D^0$, 124n38 (*see*
    also Small clauses)
Barwise, J., 120
Belletti, A., 9, 83, 118n6, 119n13, 120n16
Benincà, P., 123n32
Bennis, H., 50
Bianchi, V., 53, 124
BOC. *See* Bare Output Conditions
Boeckx, C., 127n11
Borer, H., 100
Bowers, J., 34

Brody, M., 97, 126n54
Broekhuis, H., 125n46
Burzio, L., 129n5

Canonical copular sentences, 42, 106. *See*
  also Copula; Inverse copular sentences
Cardinaletti, A., 40, 56
Carlson, G., 86
C-command,
  category/segment-based definition of, 24
  Chomsky's (1995) definition of, 116n7
  simple definition of, 19
Chierchia, G., 86, 91, 96, 98, 99, 121n23
Chomsky, N., 2, 4, 5, 6, 7, 8, 9, 10, 11,
  12, 13, 24, 26, 30, 32, 33, 34, 36, 40, 41,
  43, 54, 87, 96, 97, 100, 111, 115n2,
  116n7, 117n11, 117n3, 118n6, 119n13,
  126n54, 127n6, 127n8, 129n7, 130n9,
  130n11
ci,
  and the lexicalization of the copula, 112
  as a raised predicate, 109–110 (*see also*
    Existential sentences; *it*; *there*)
Cinque, G., 26, 34, 50, 59, 82, 117n9,
  119n14, 122n29, 129n5, 129n7, 130n12
Clitics,
  clitic movement as a neutralization of a
    point of symmetry, 85
  clitic movement in a Northern Italian
    dialect, 89–90
  the representation of clitics, 85–88 (*see*
    also Head-head constructions)
Cooper, R., 120n17
Copular sentences. *See* Canonical copular
  sentences; Copula; Inverse copular
  sentences
Copula,
  against the analysis of the copula as a
    predicate of identity, 127n2
  as the expression of the I^0 system, 120n4